This Book Belongs To:

_____

- -

_____

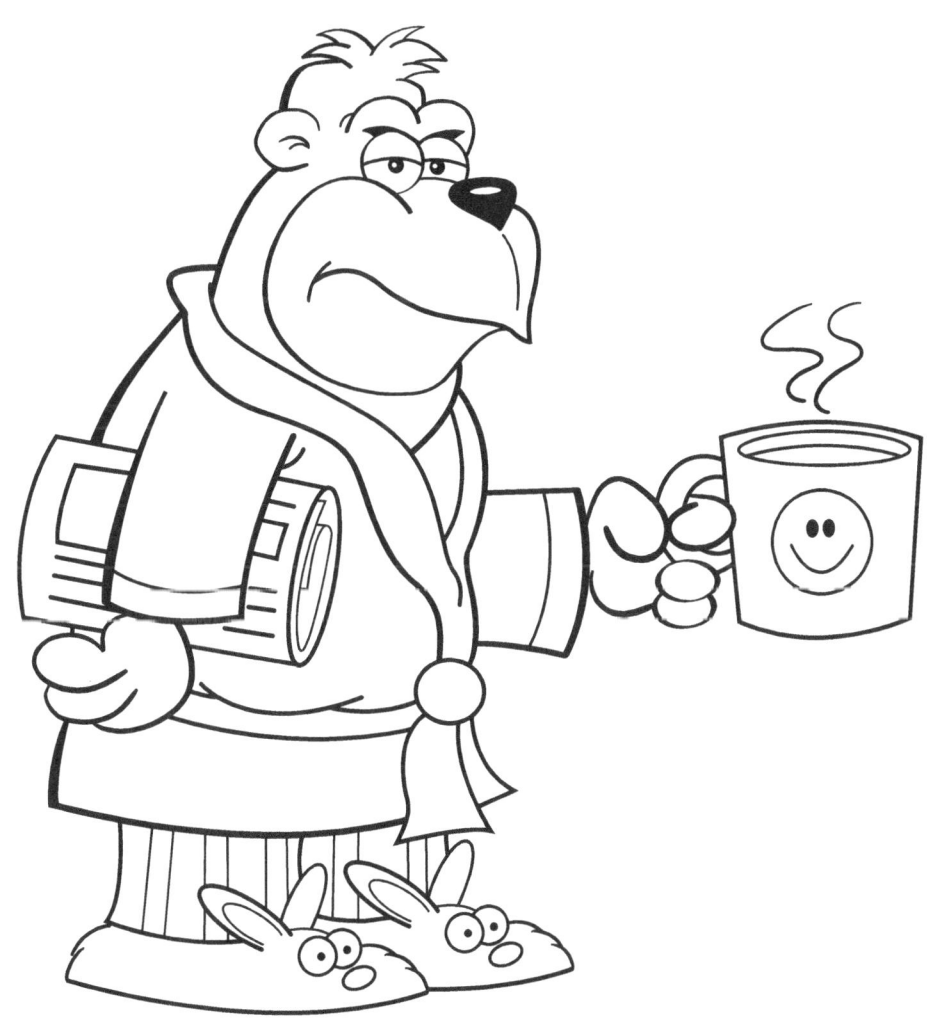

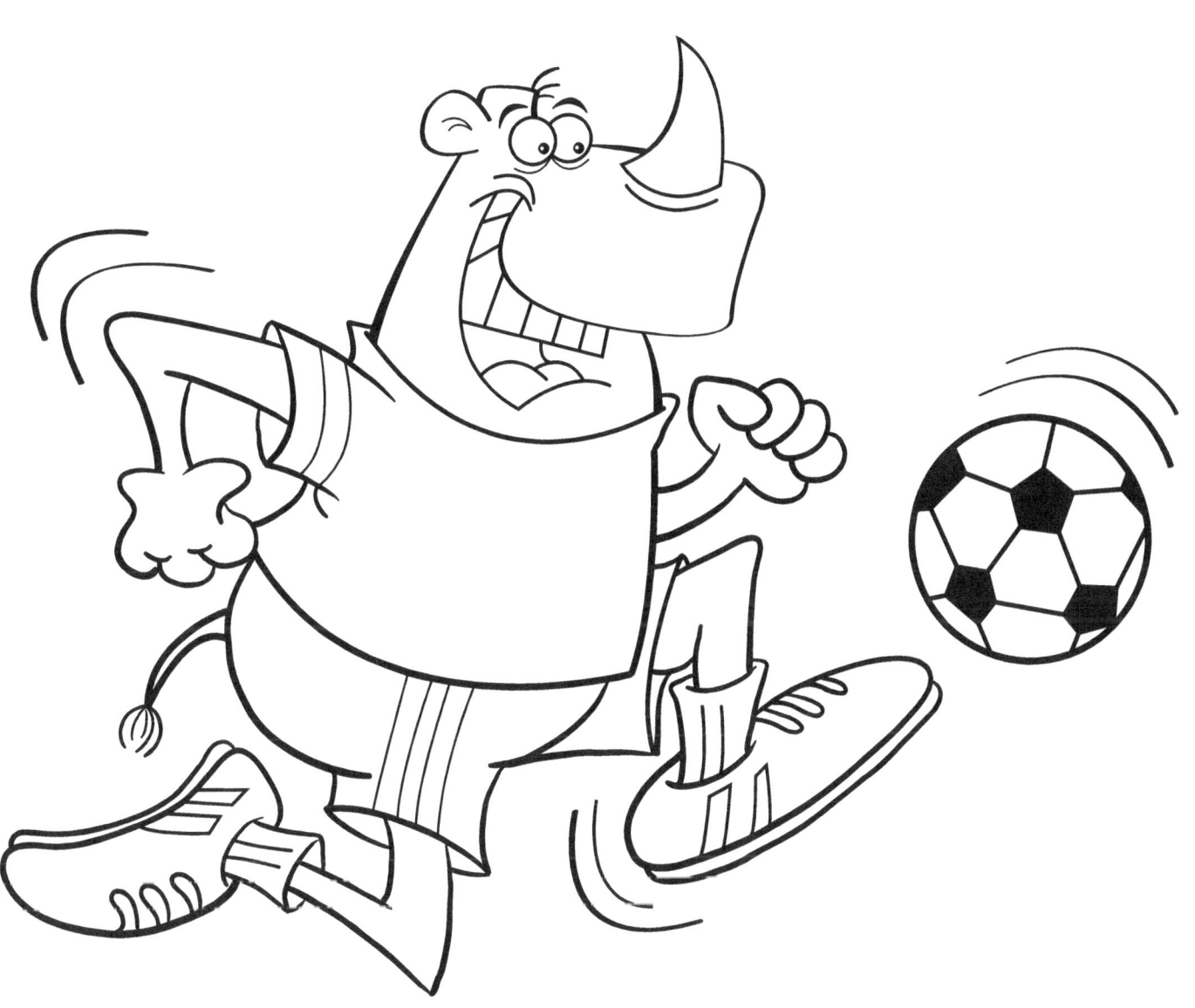

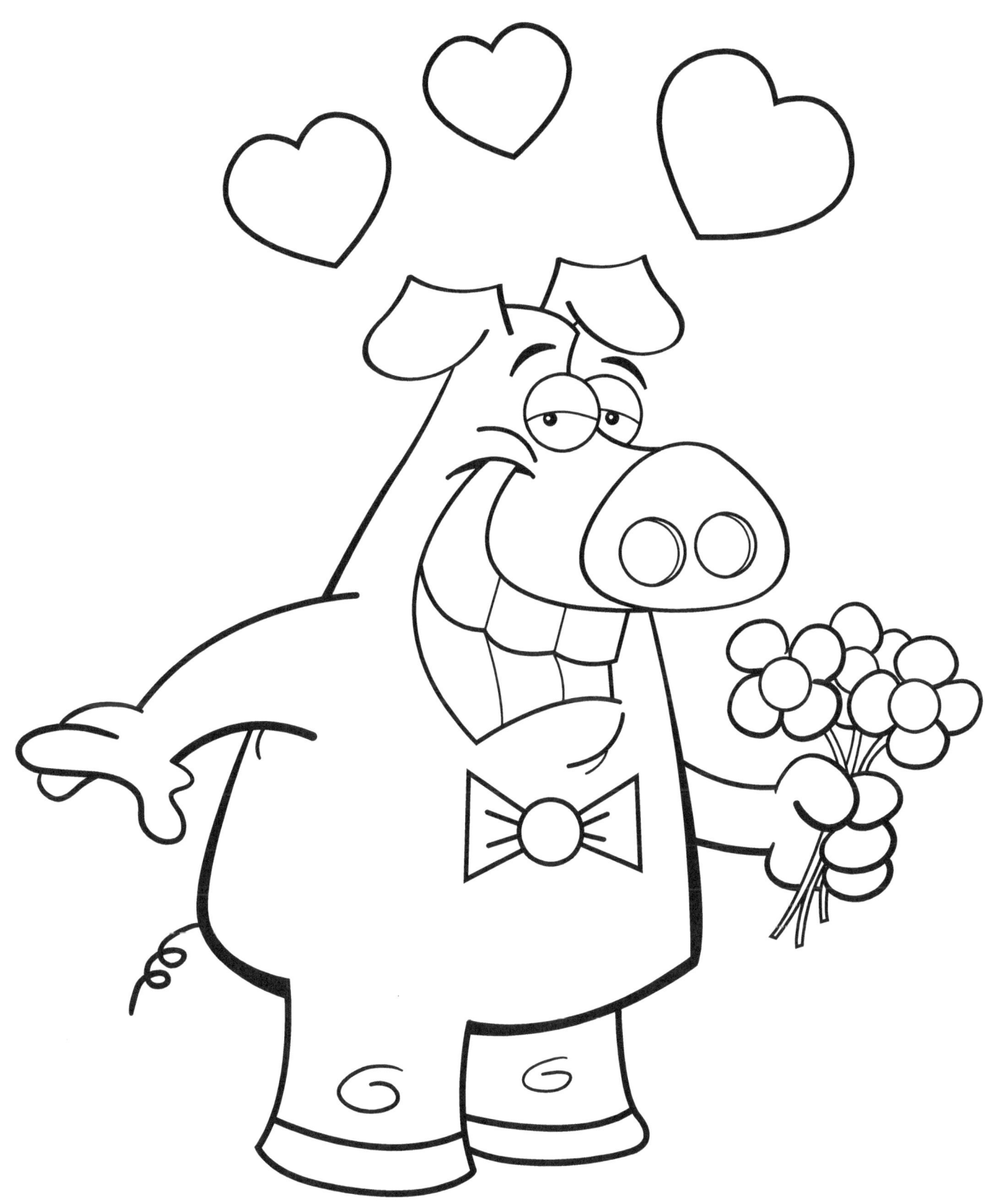

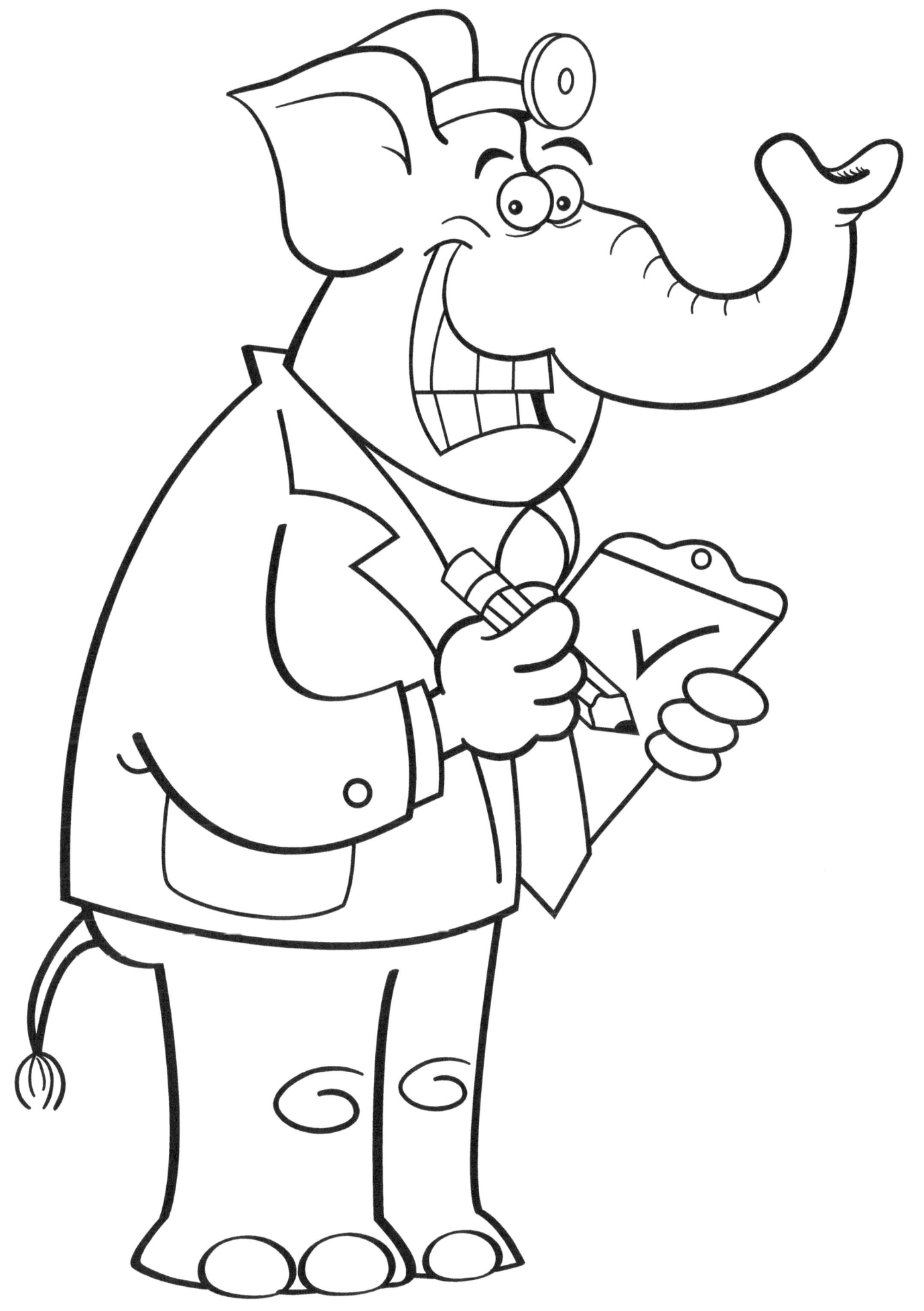

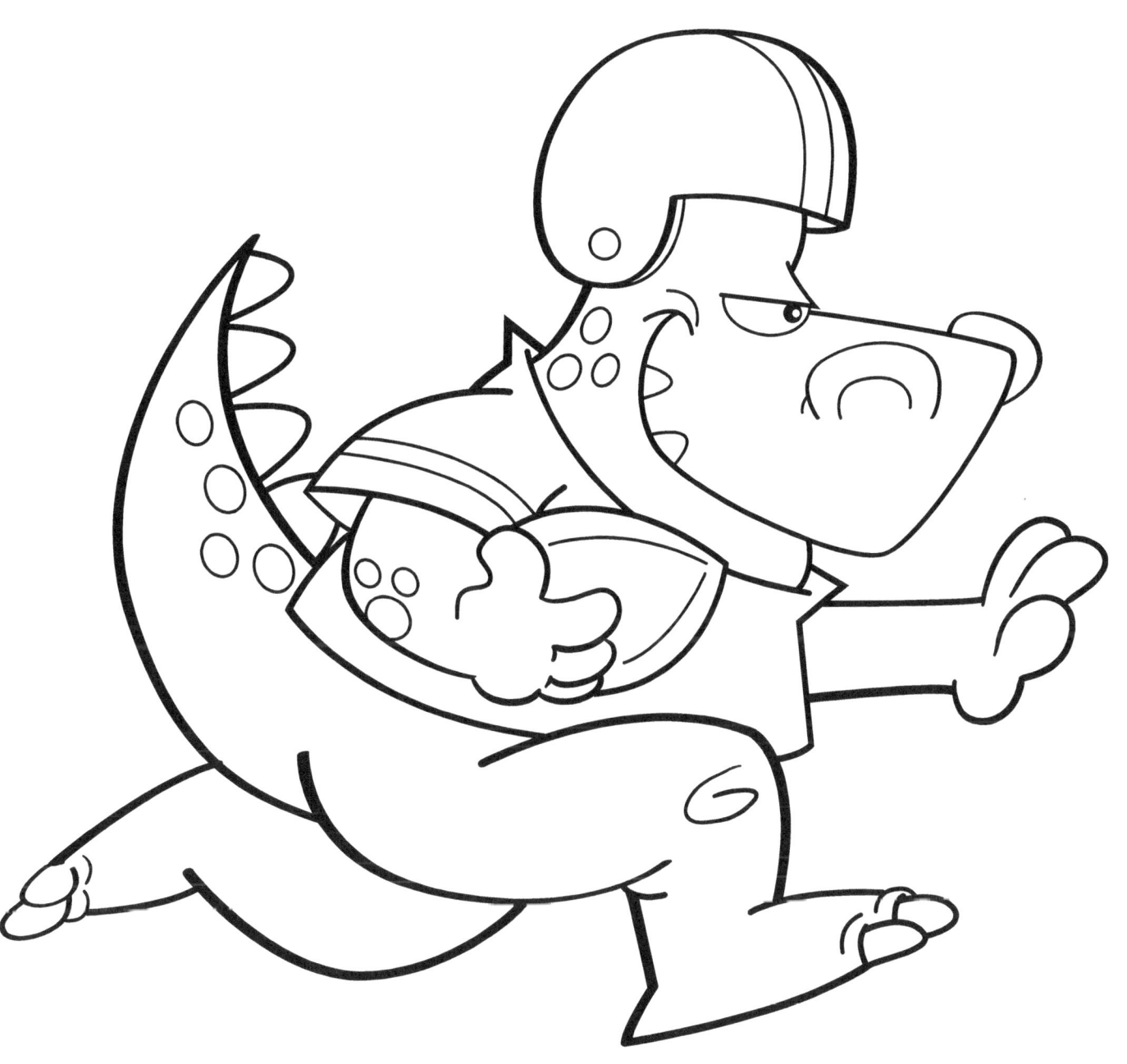

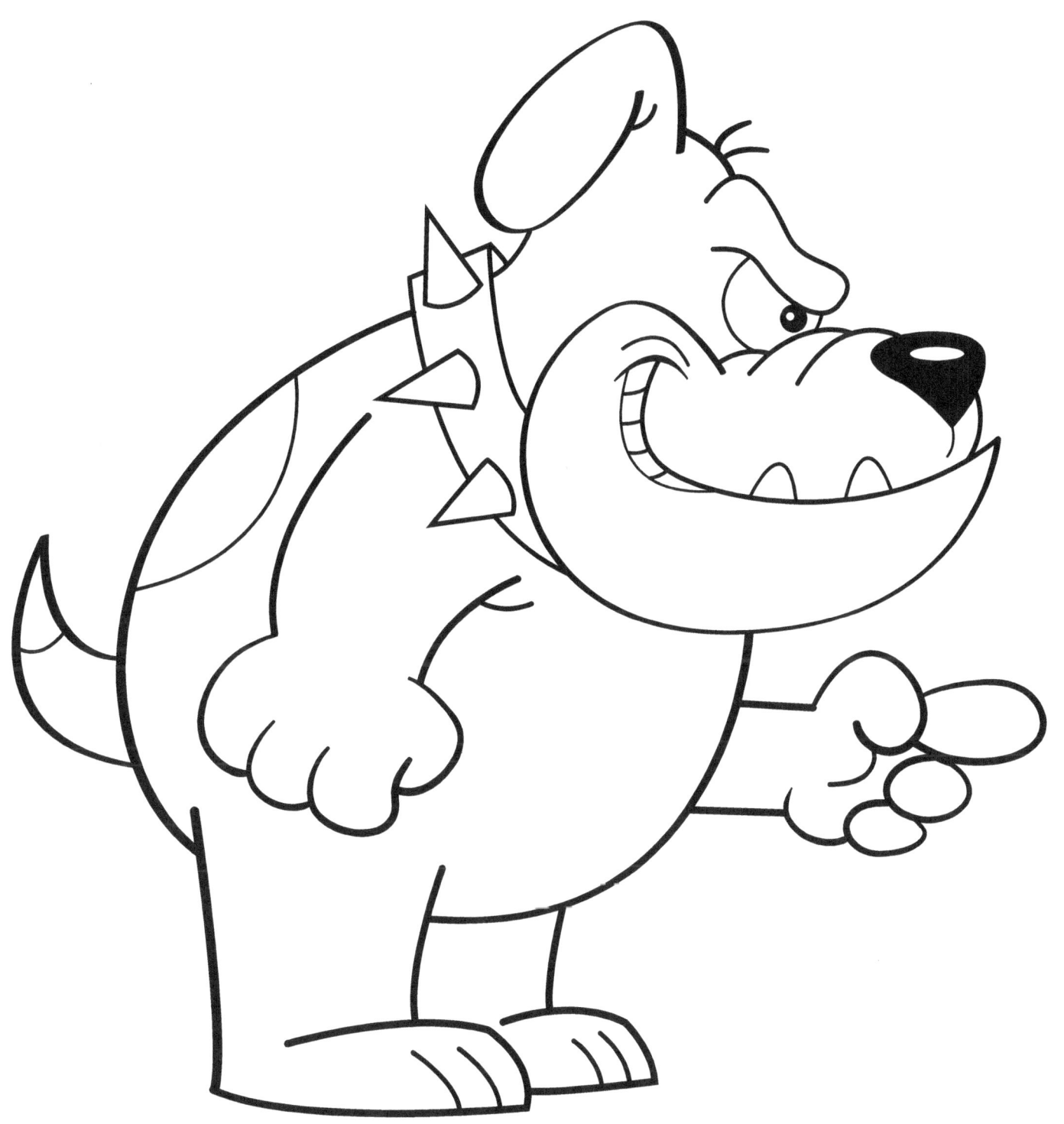

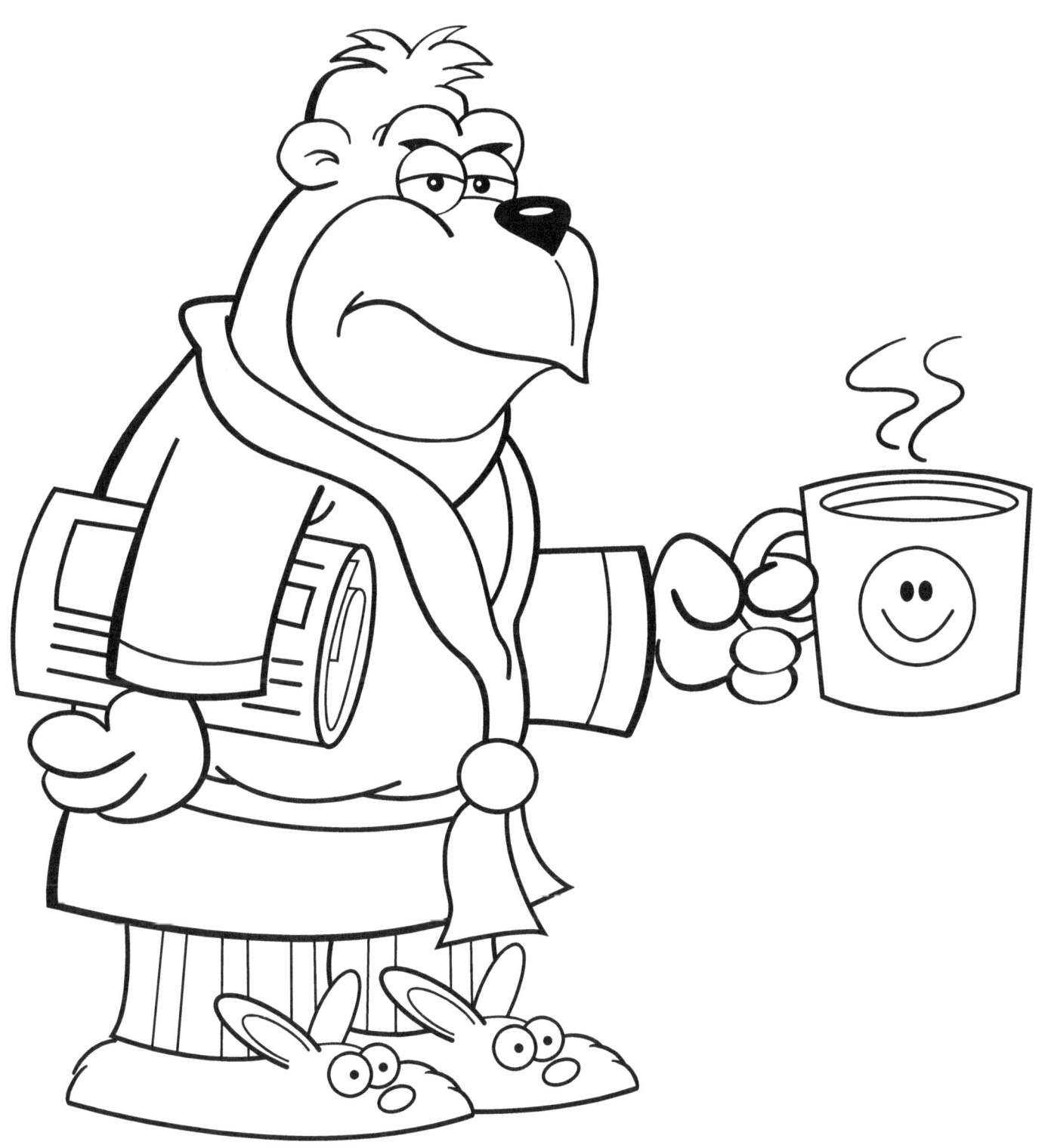

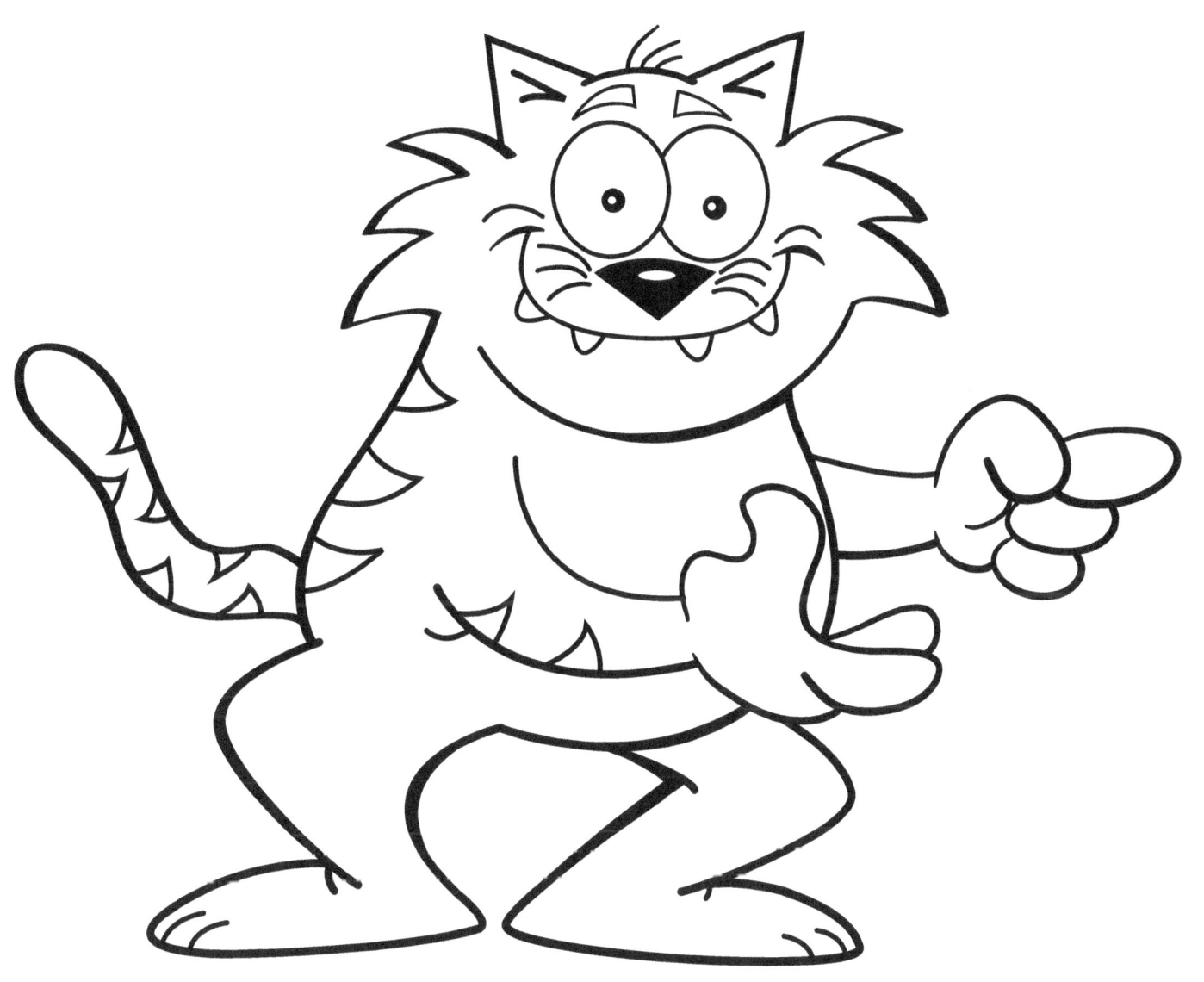

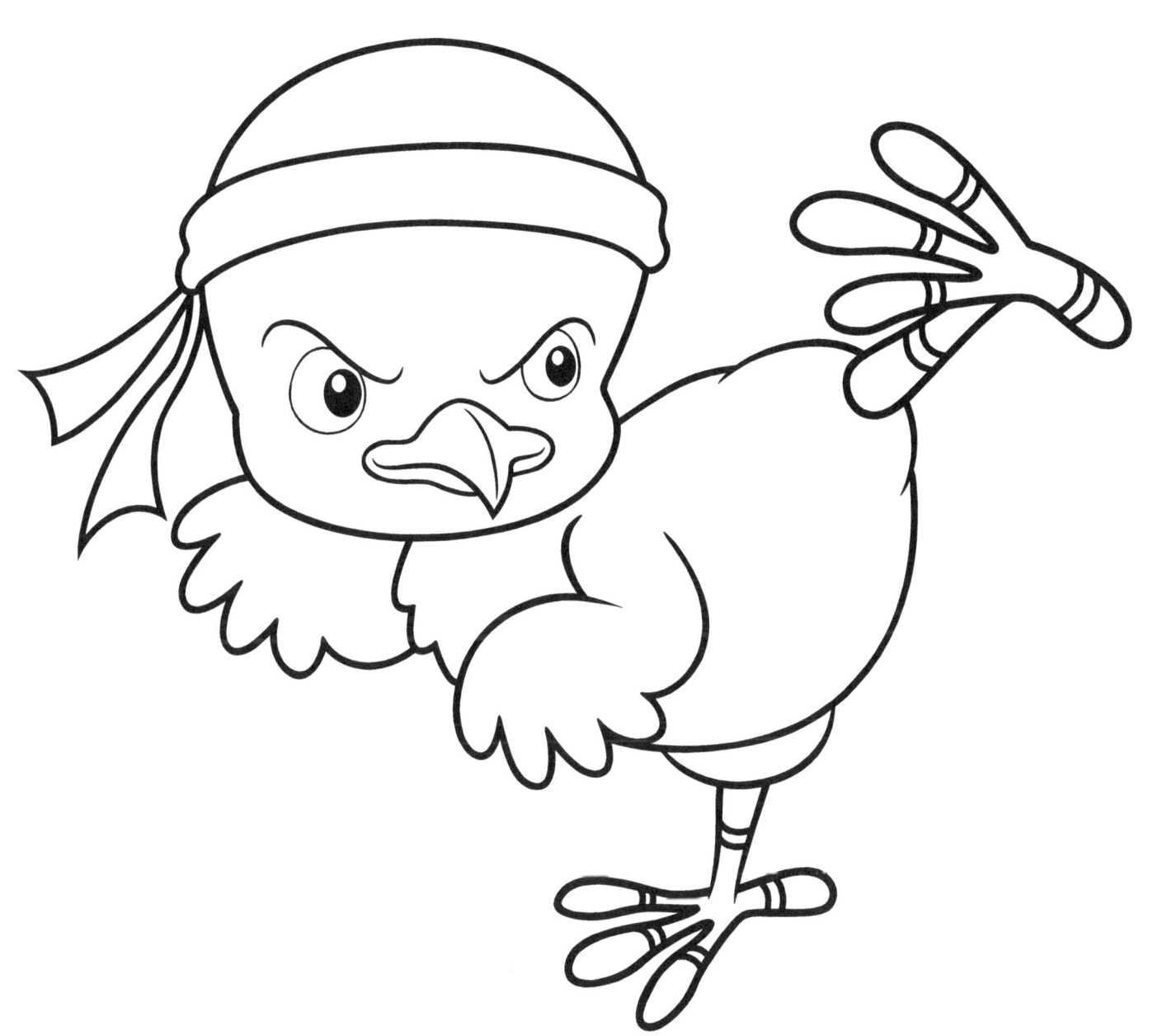

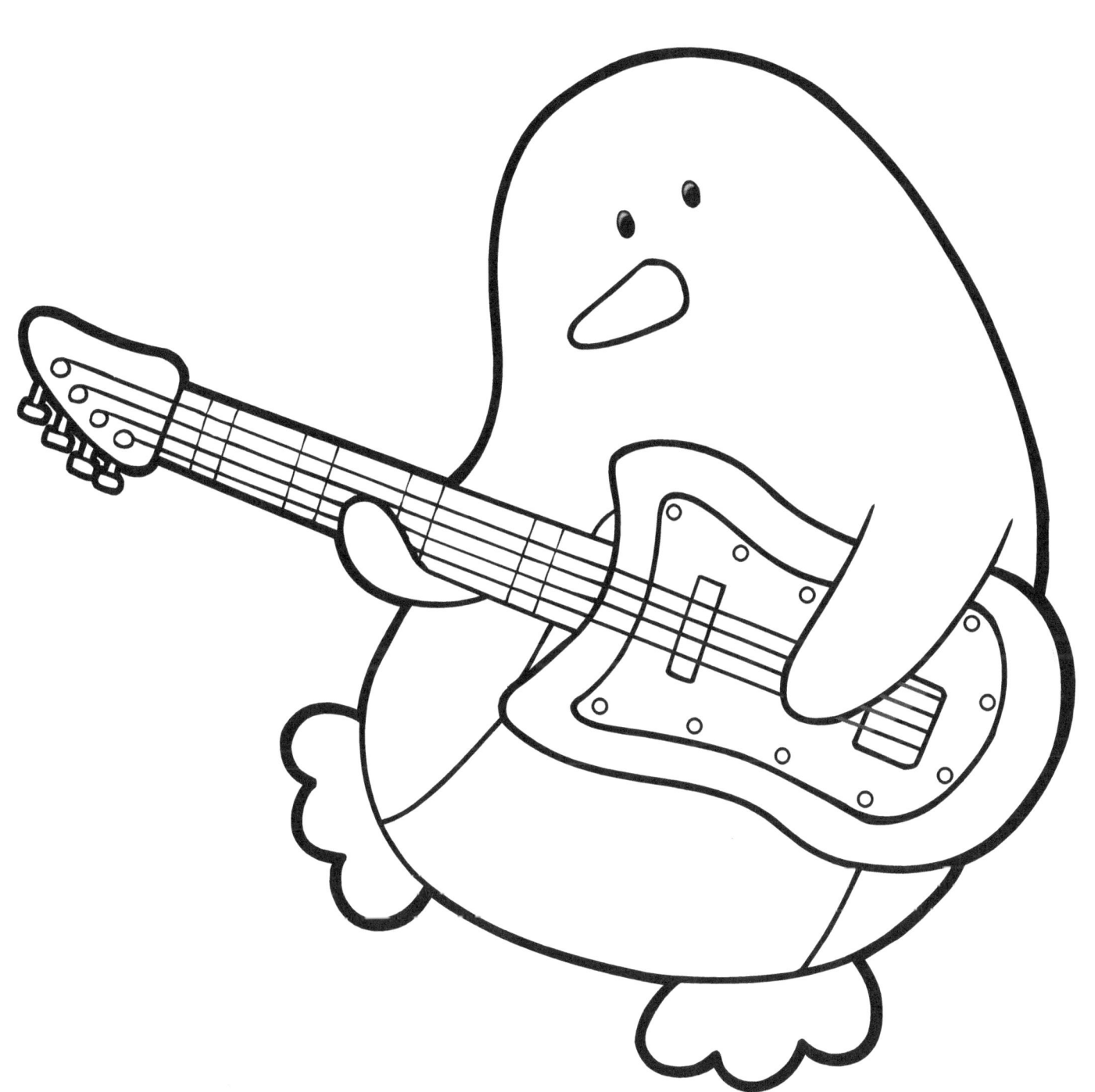

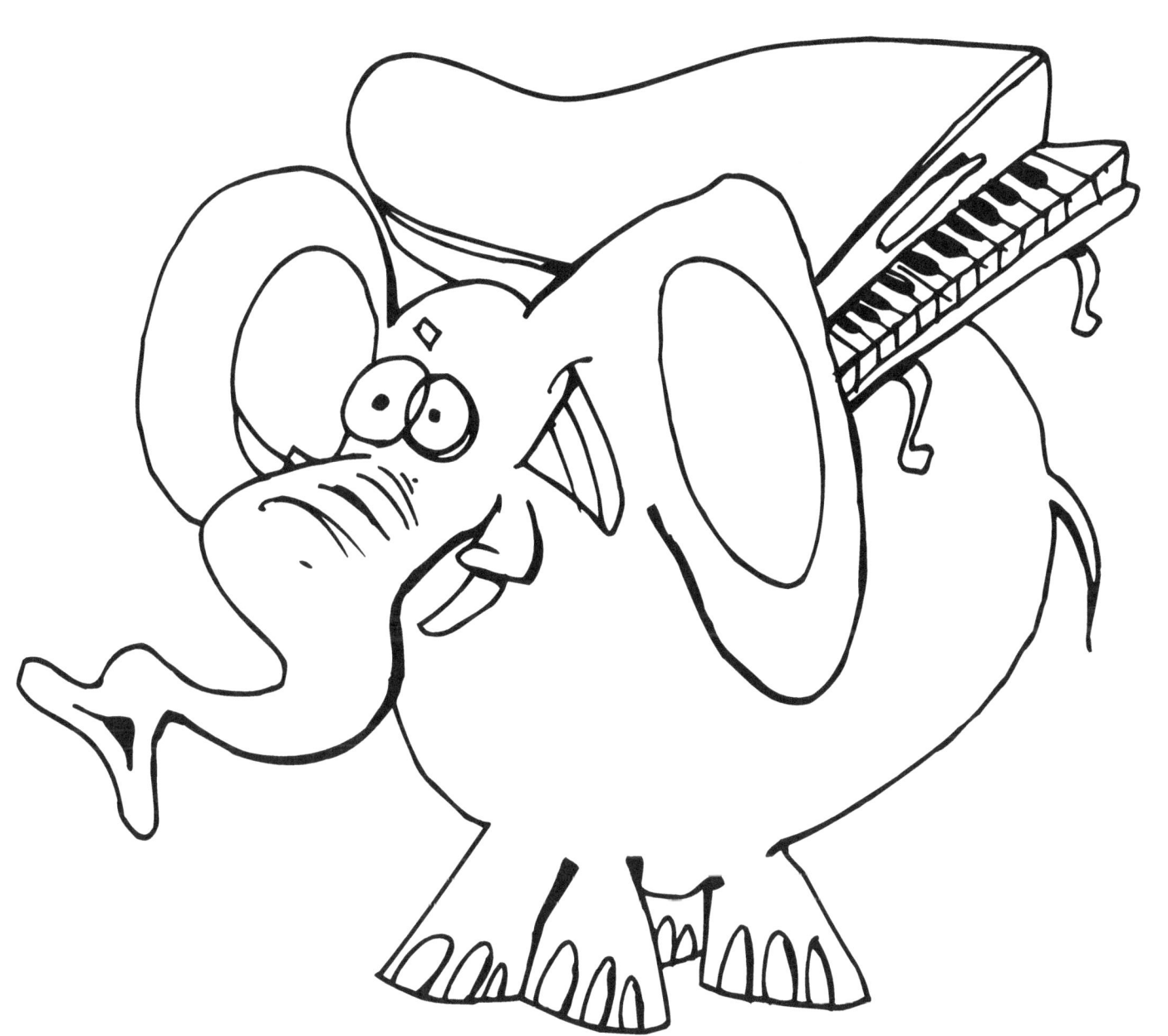

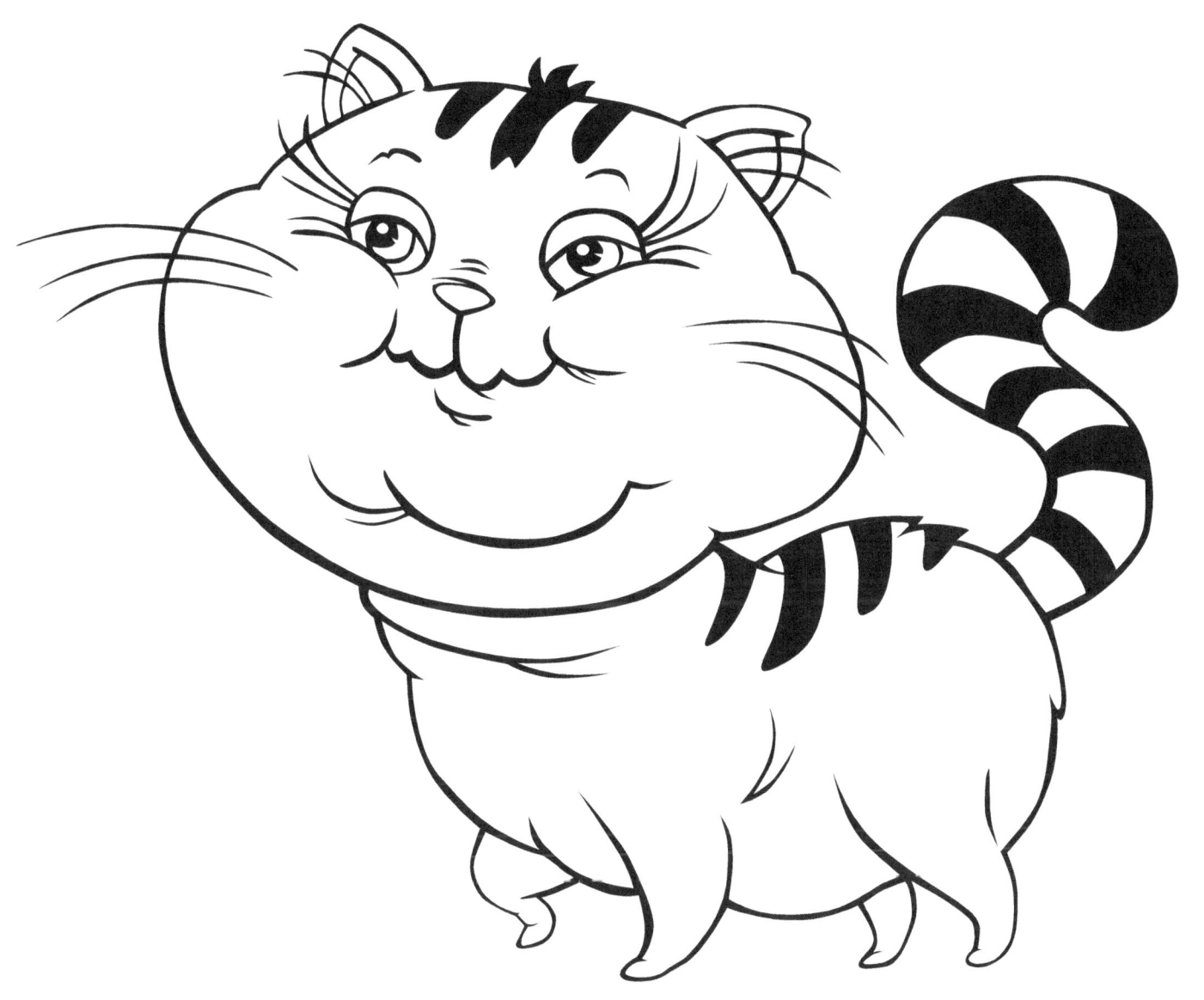

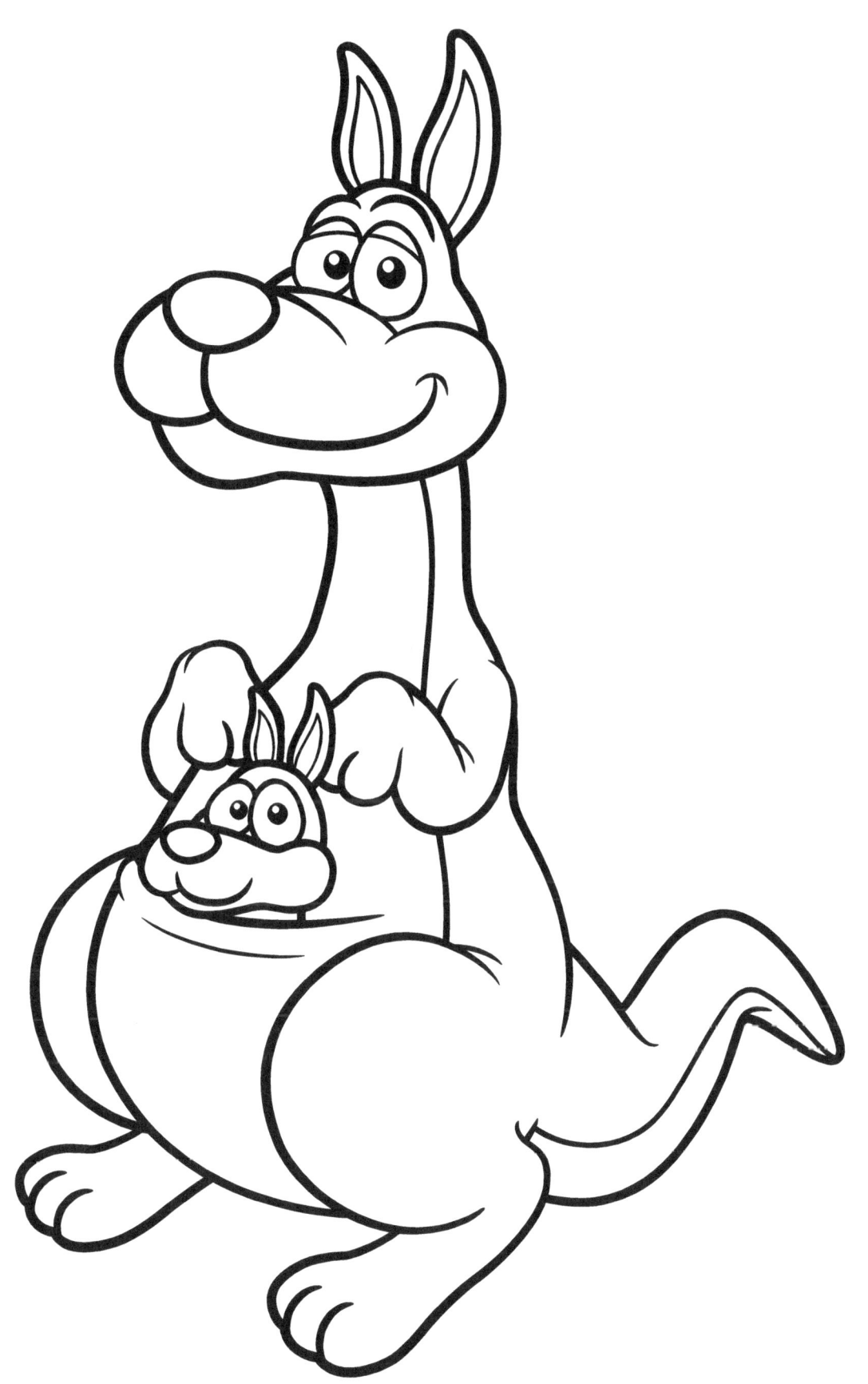

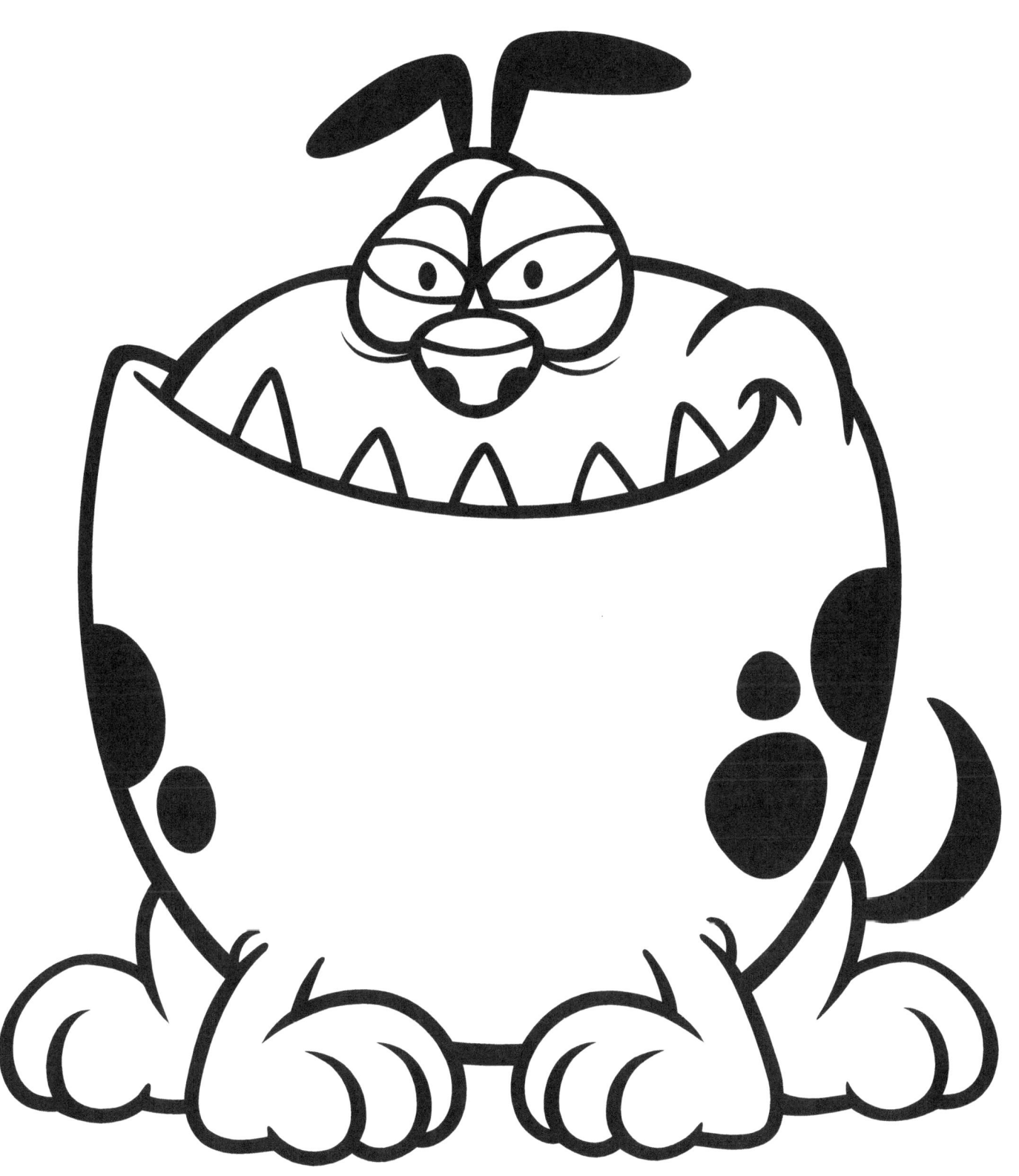

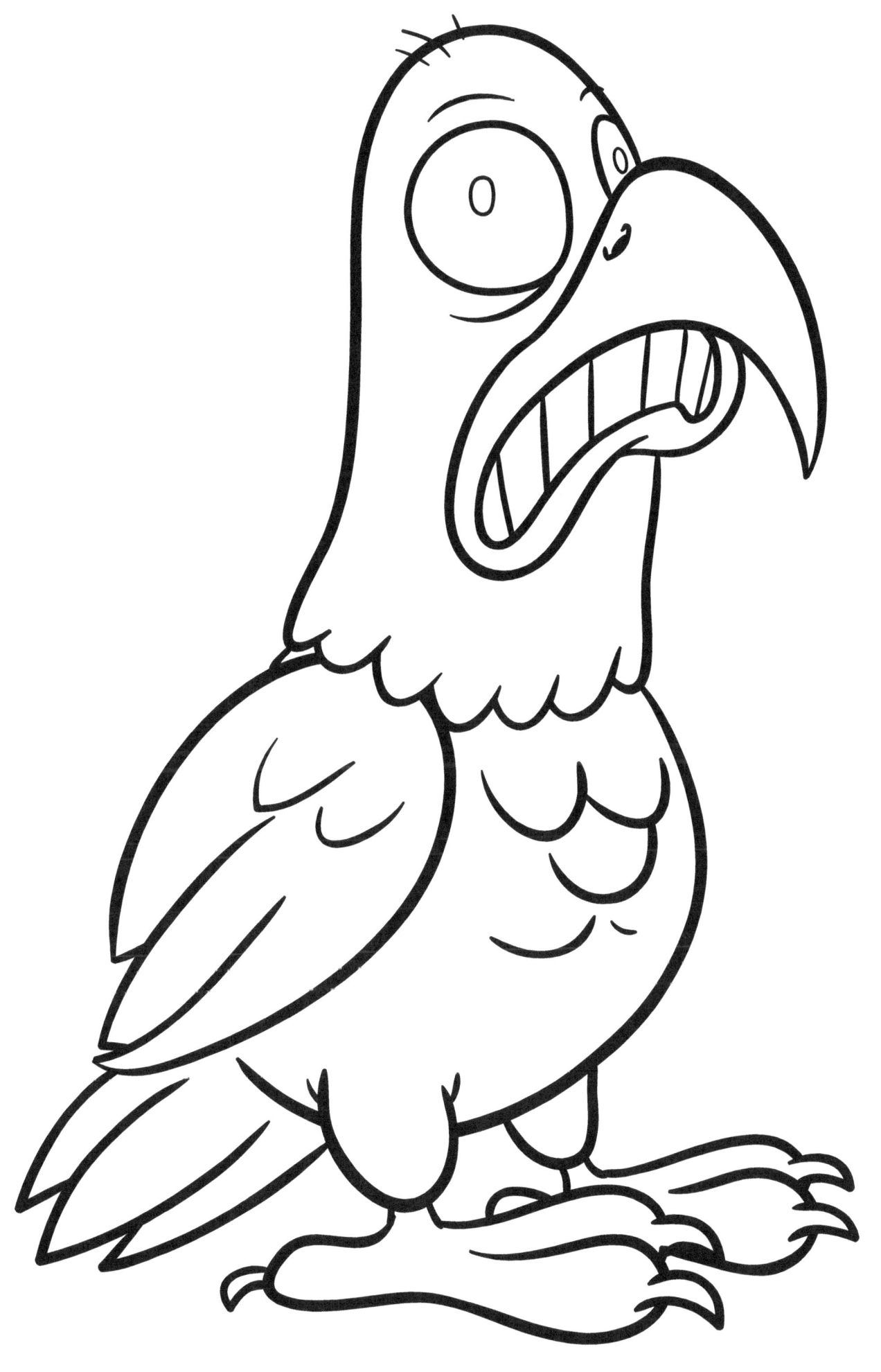

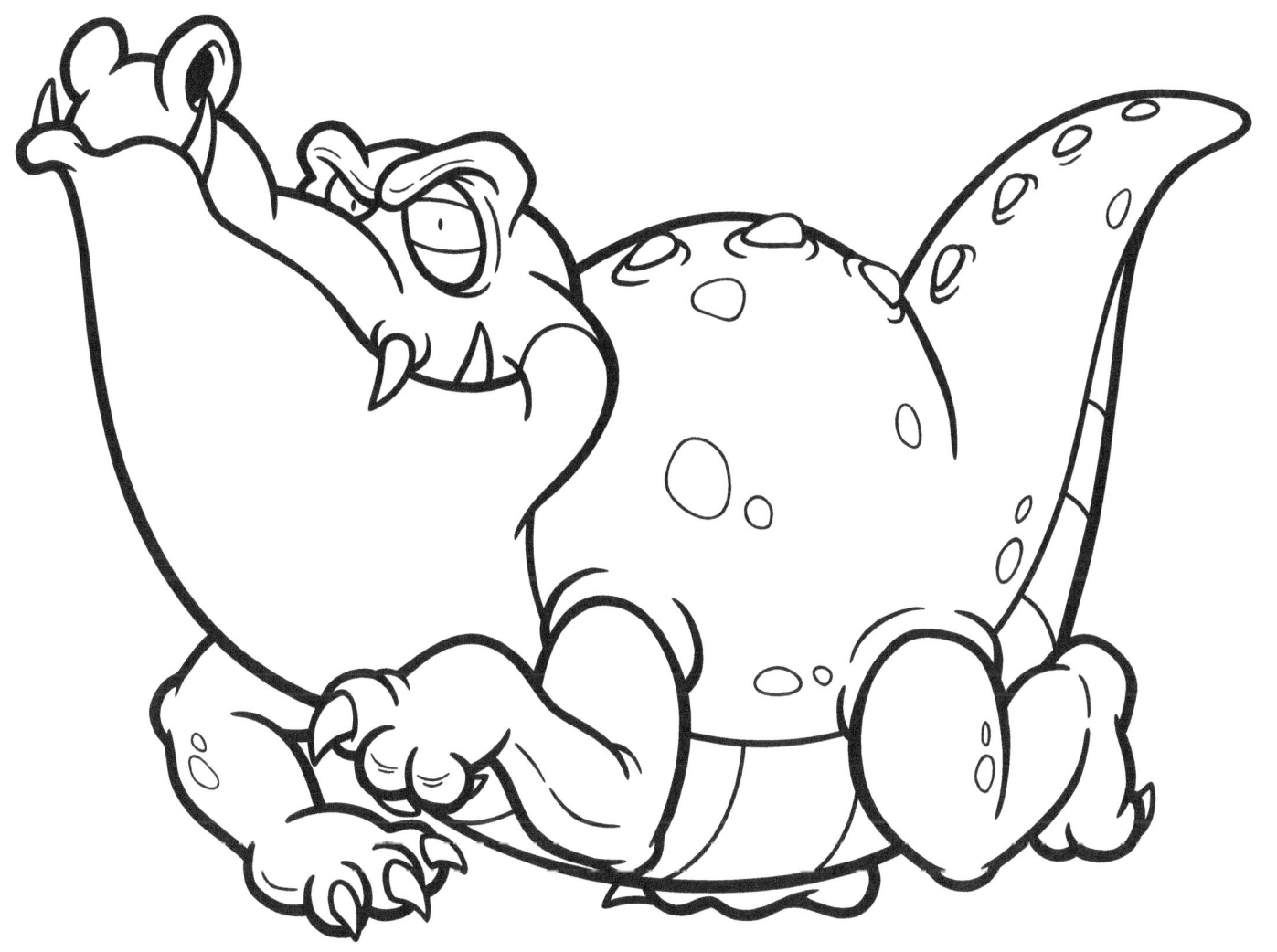

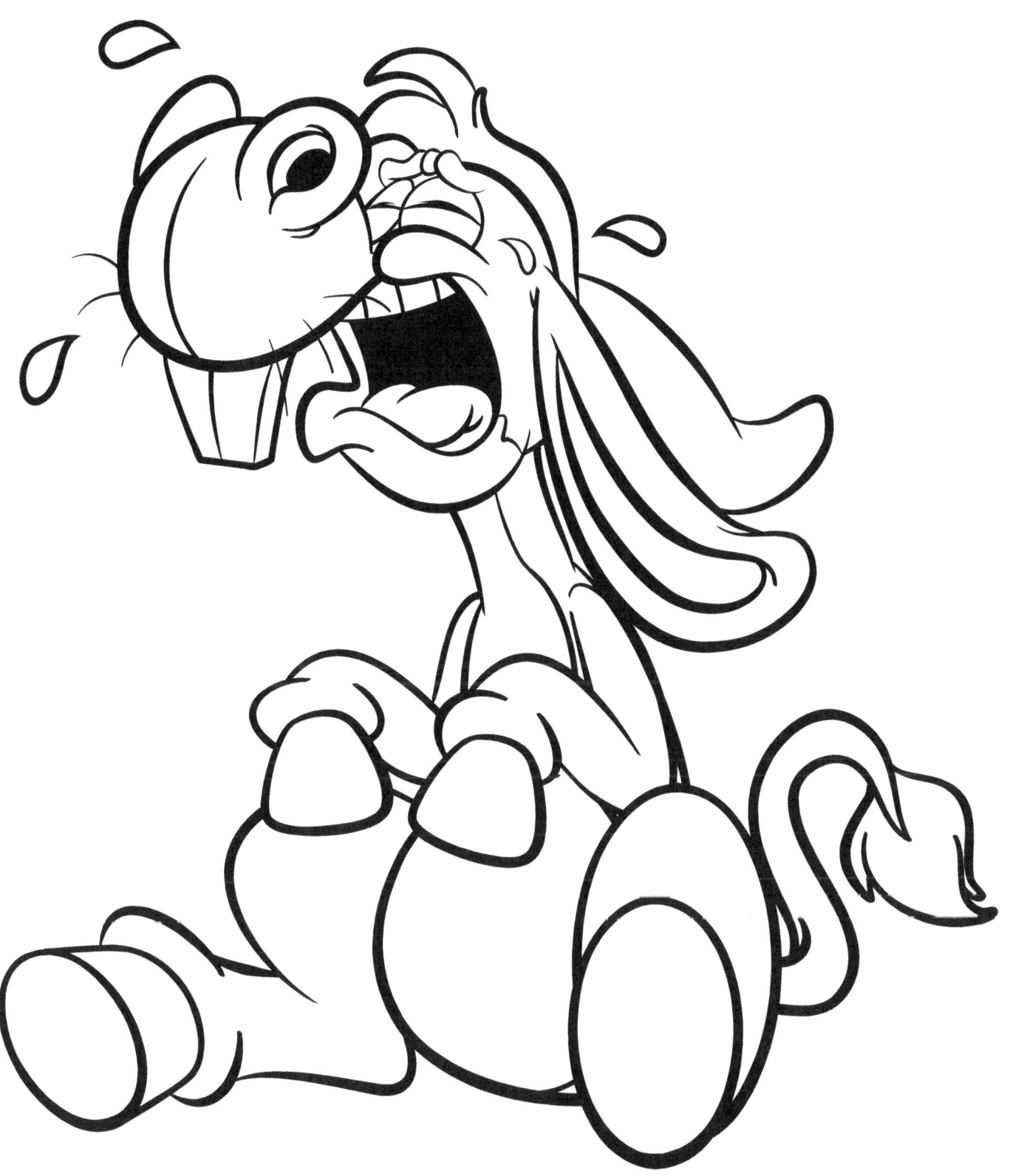

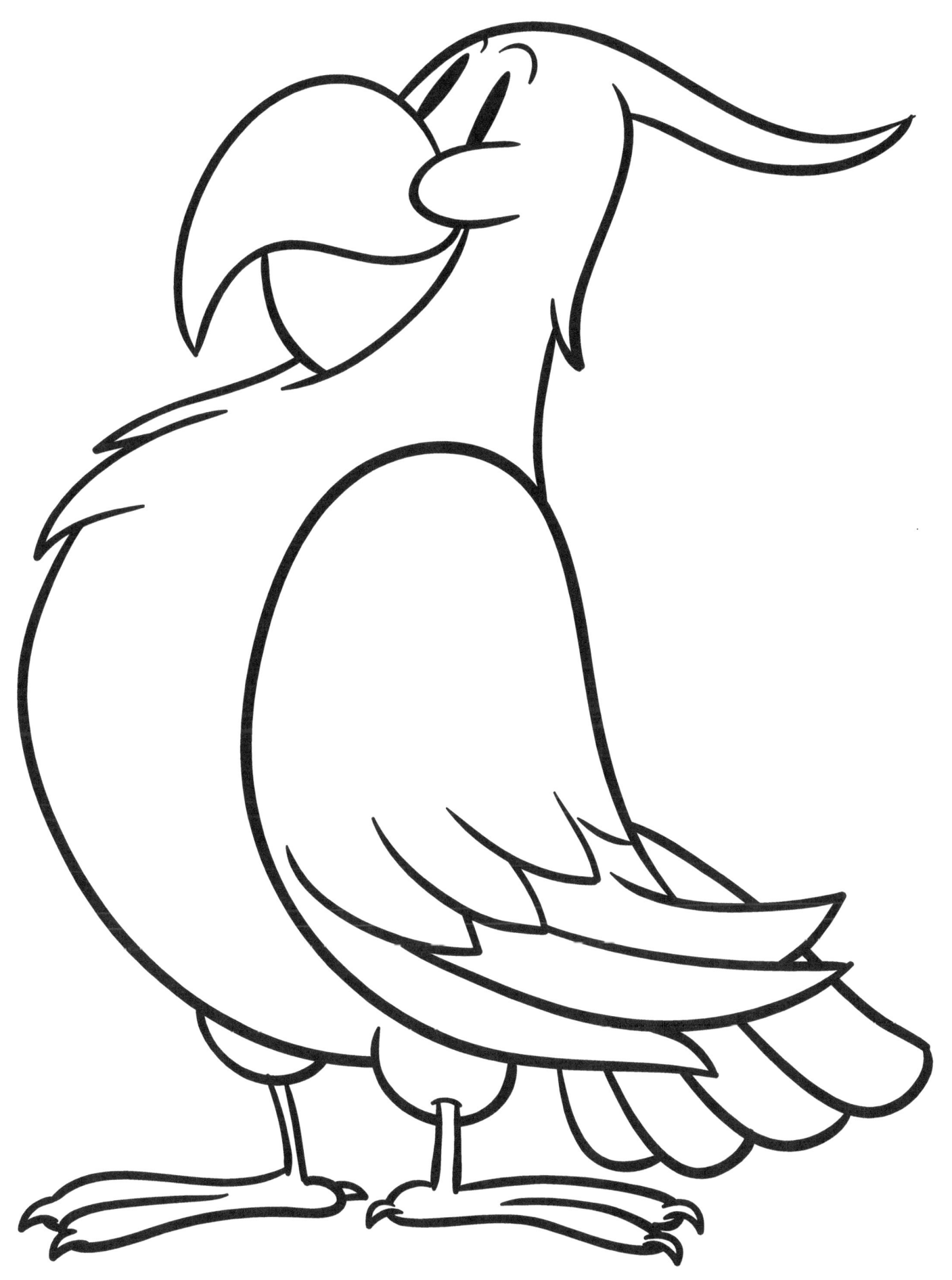

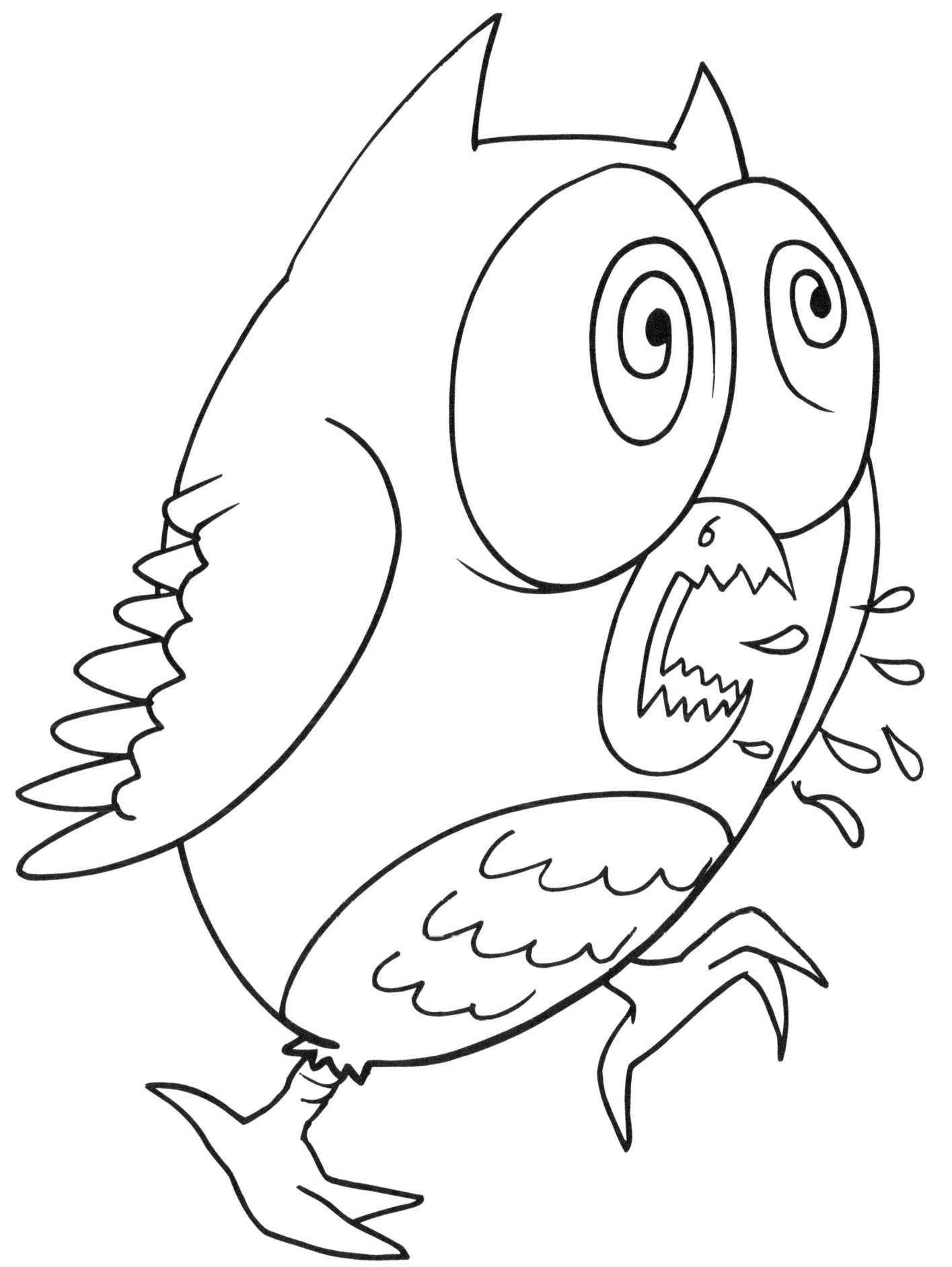

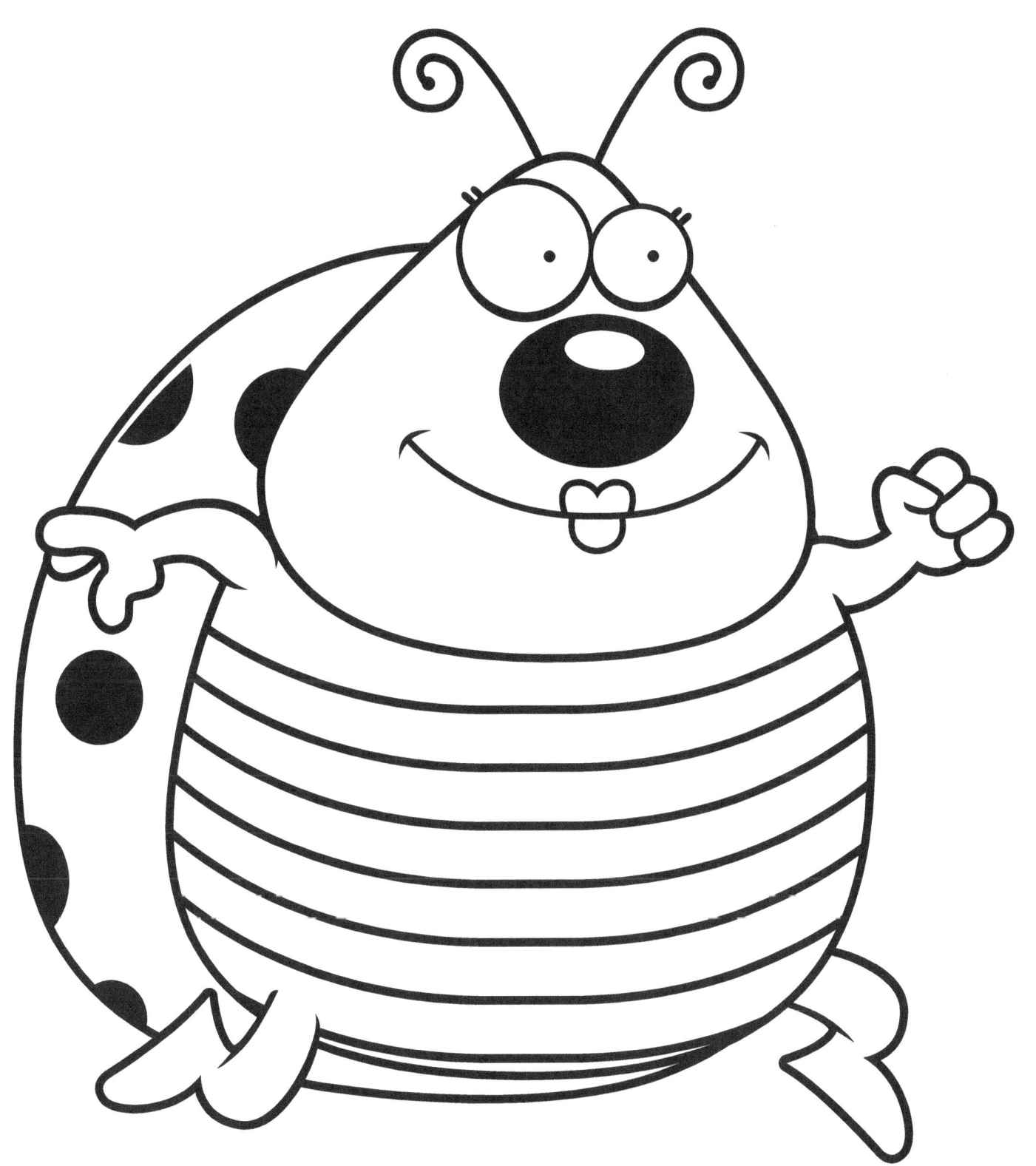

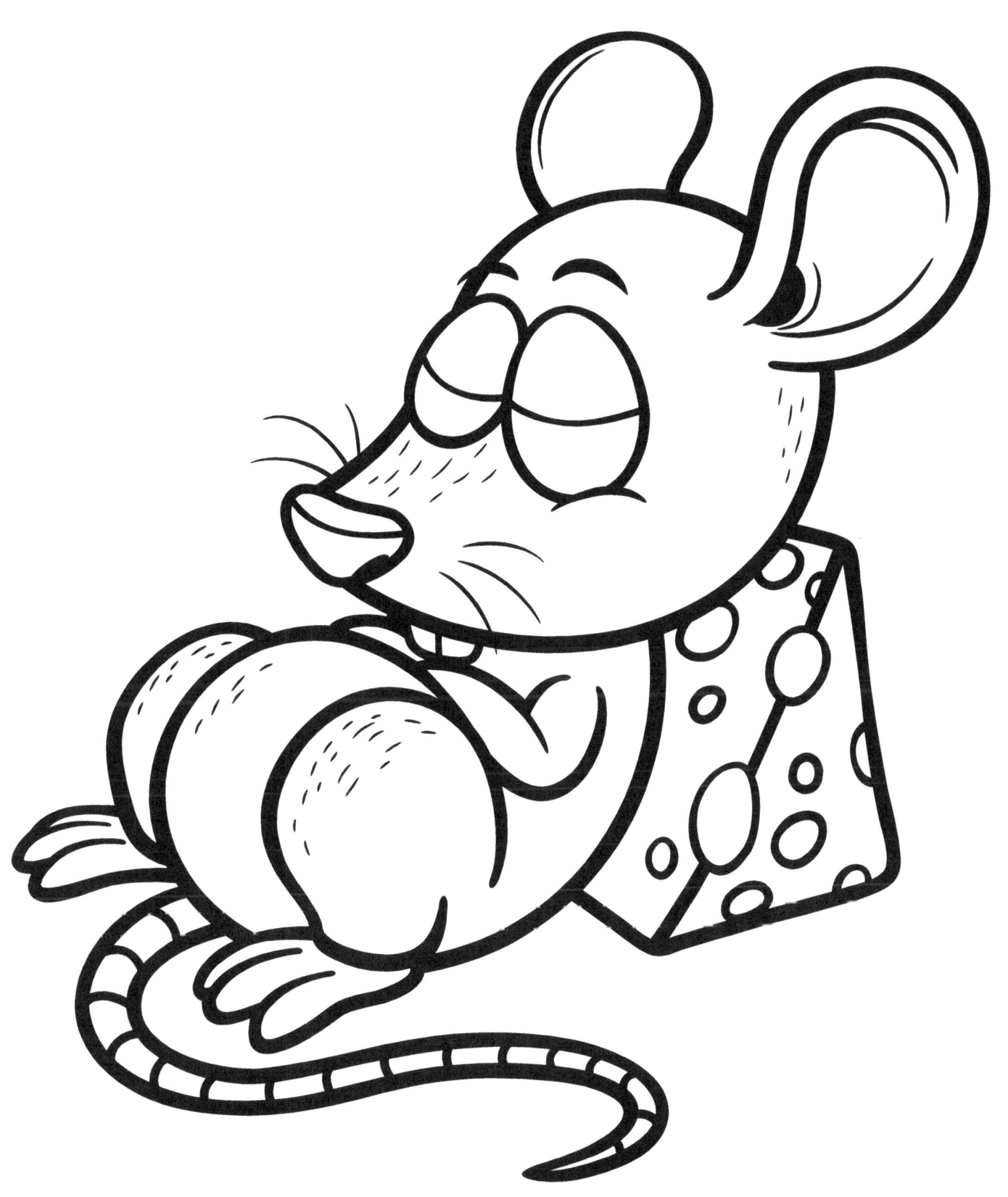

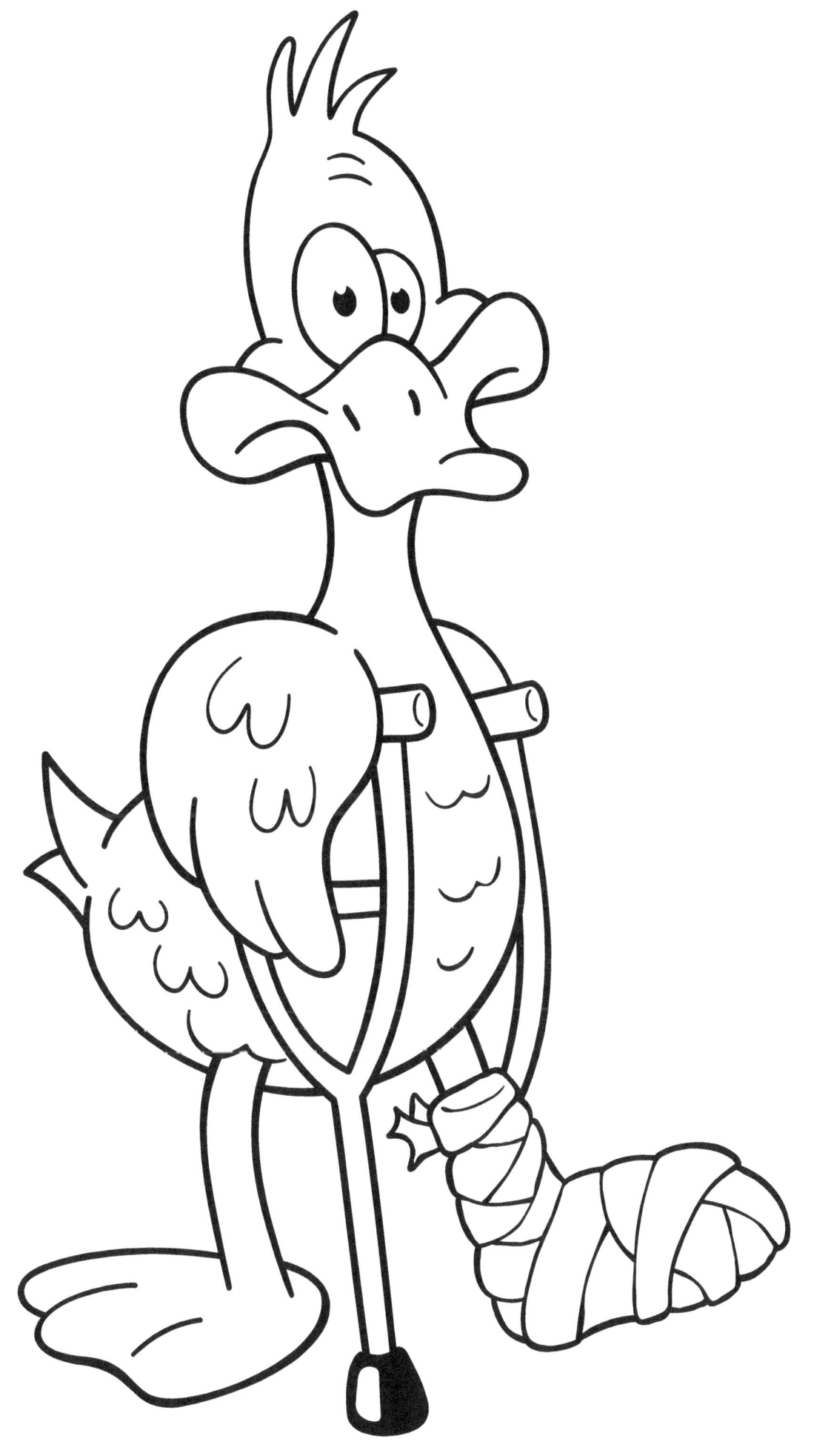

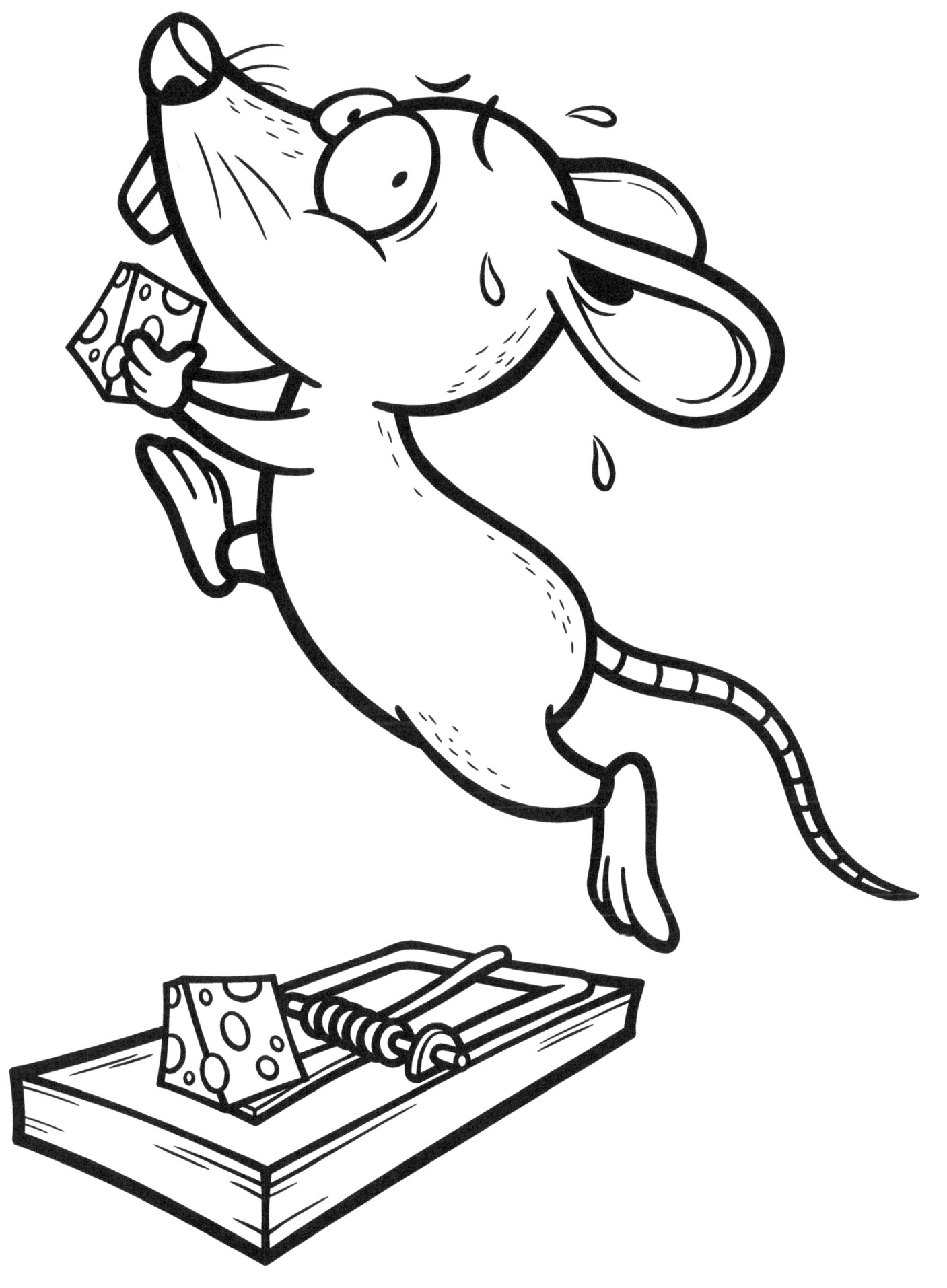

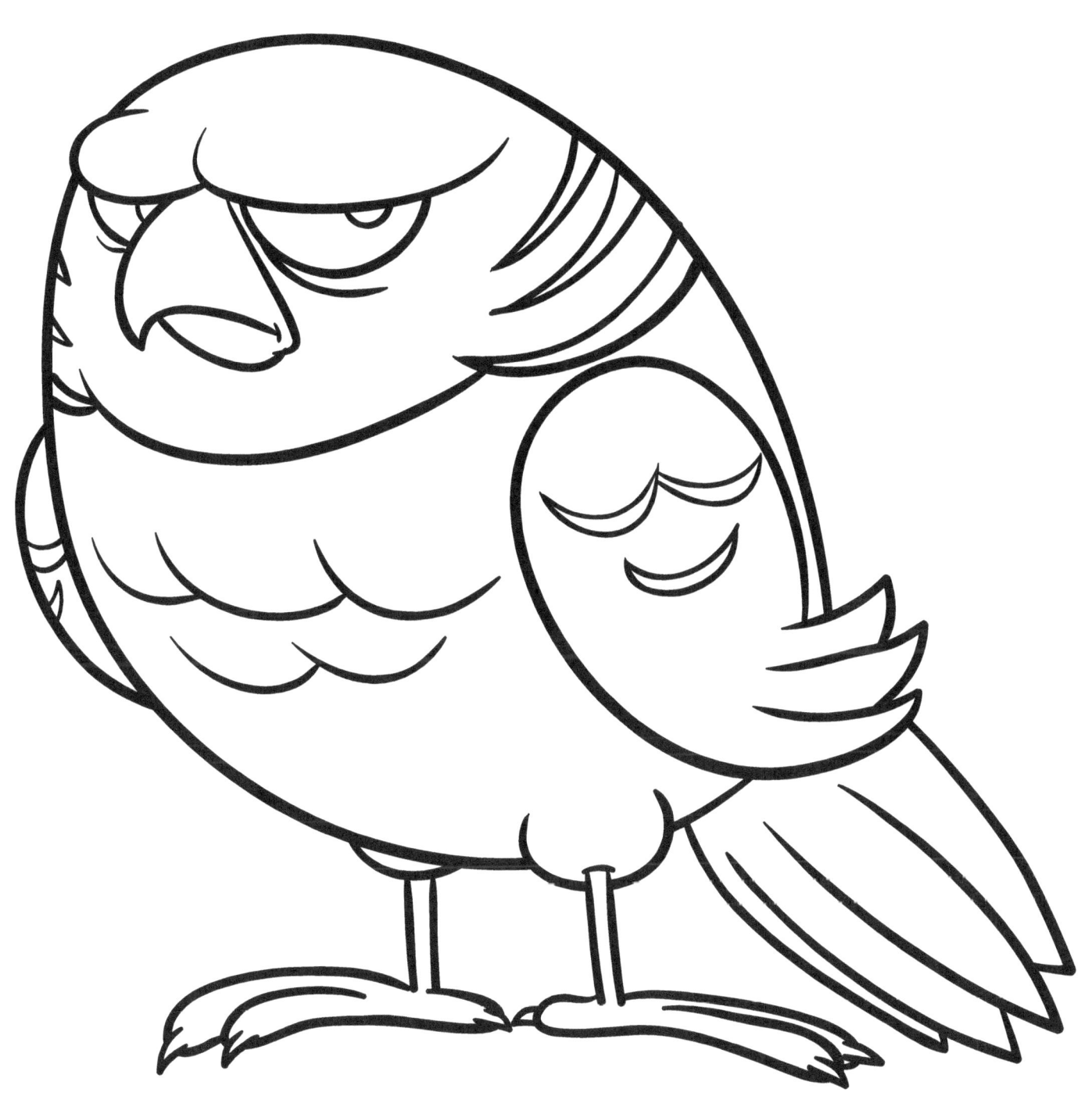

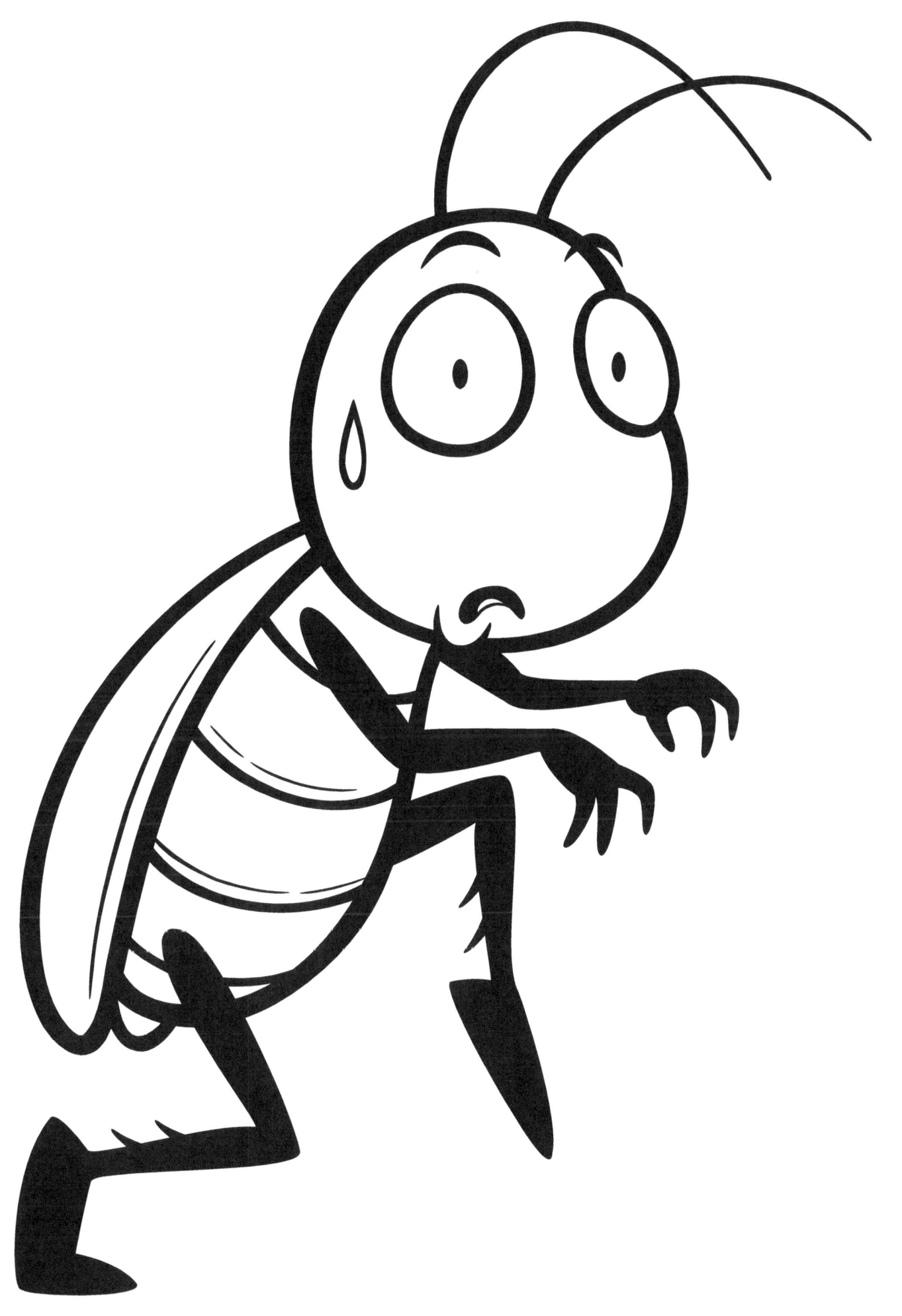

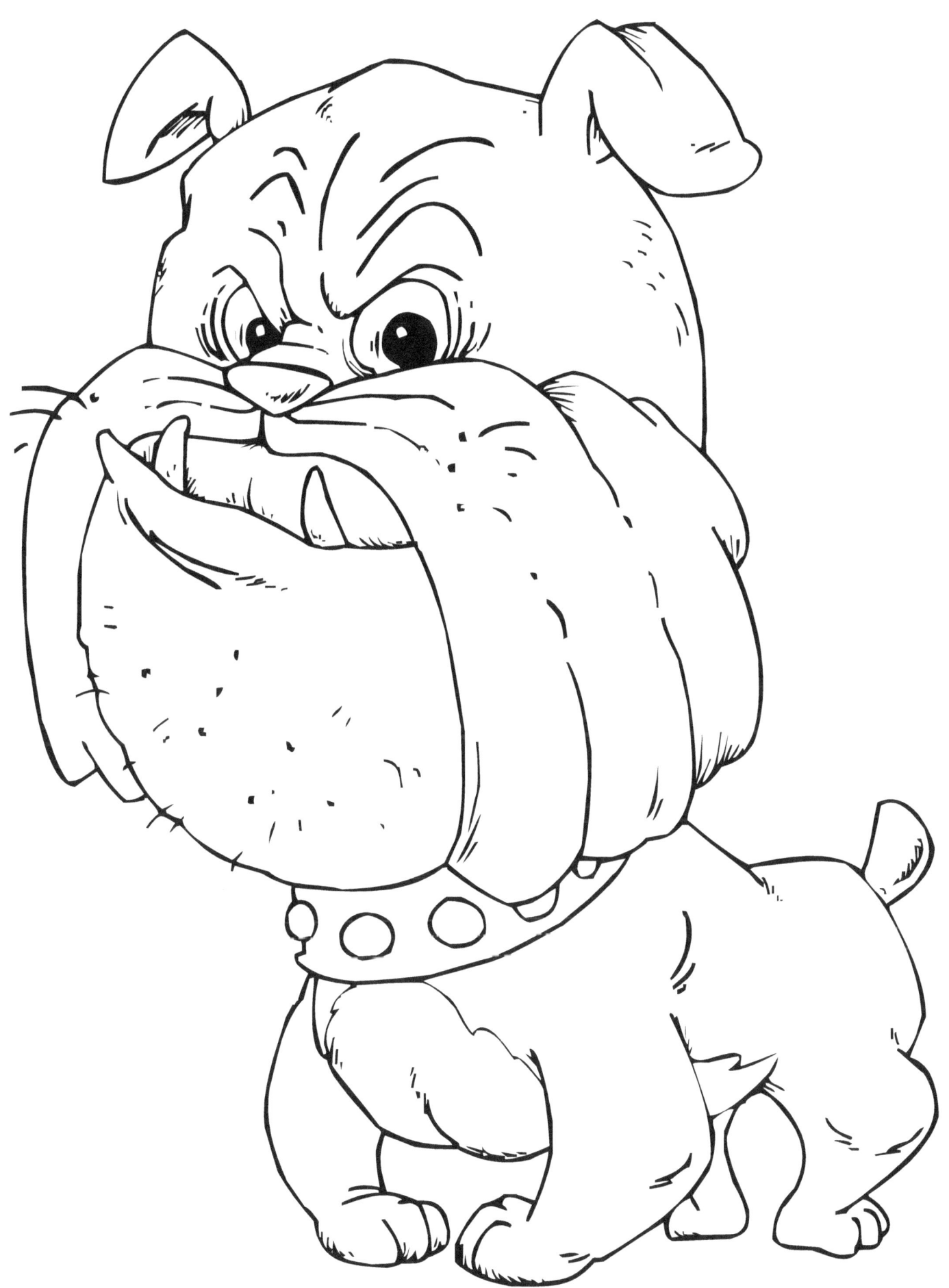

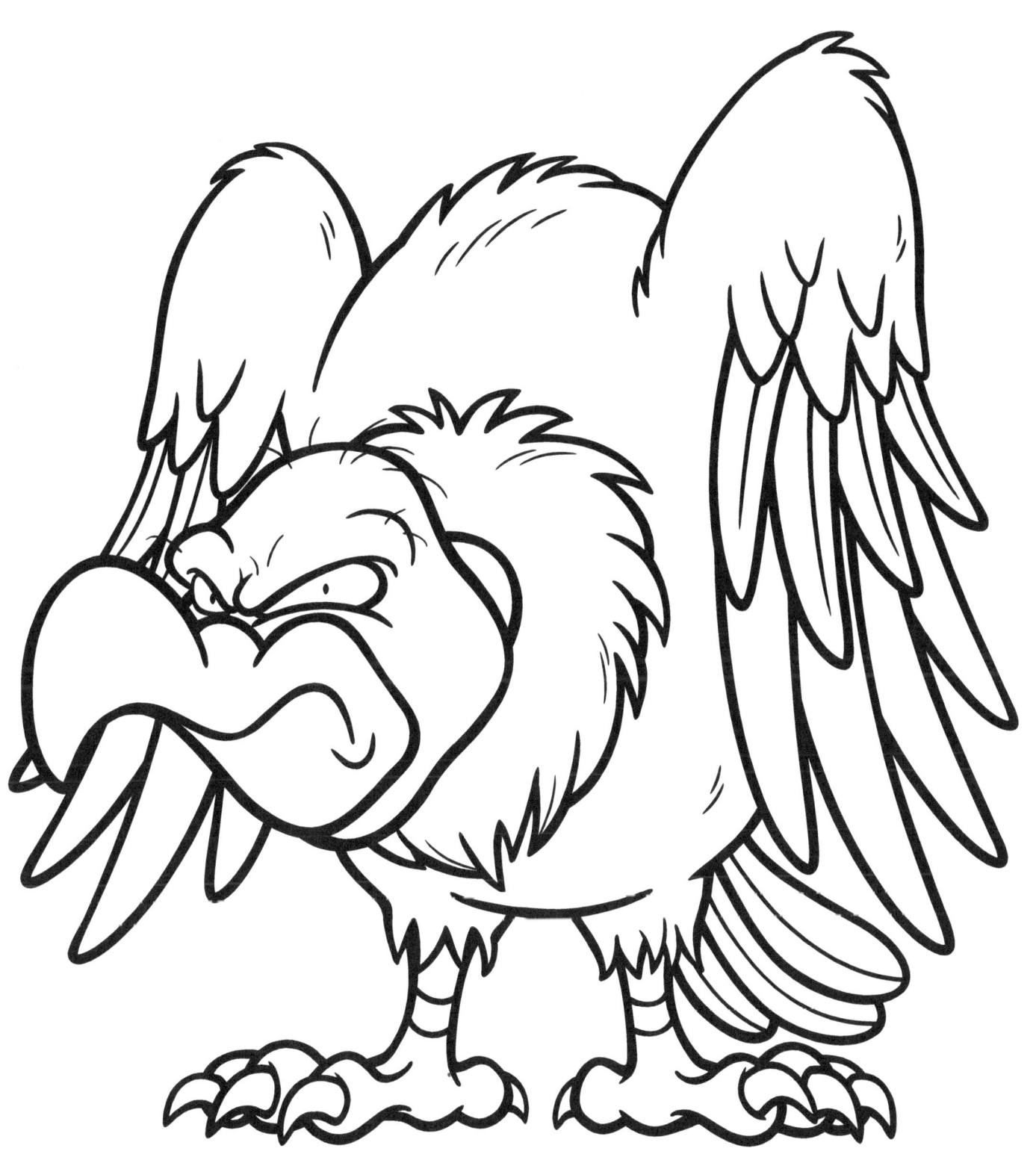

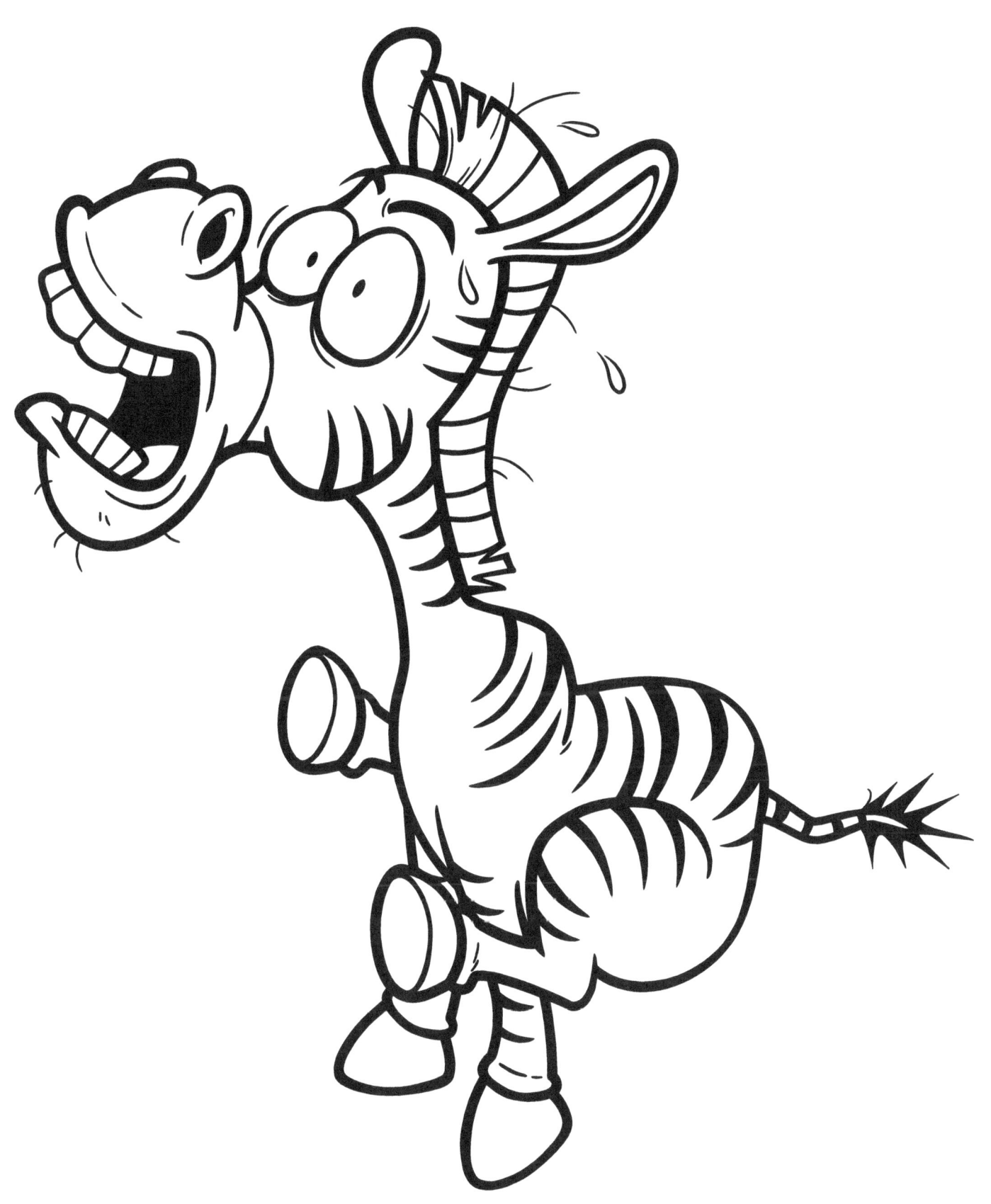

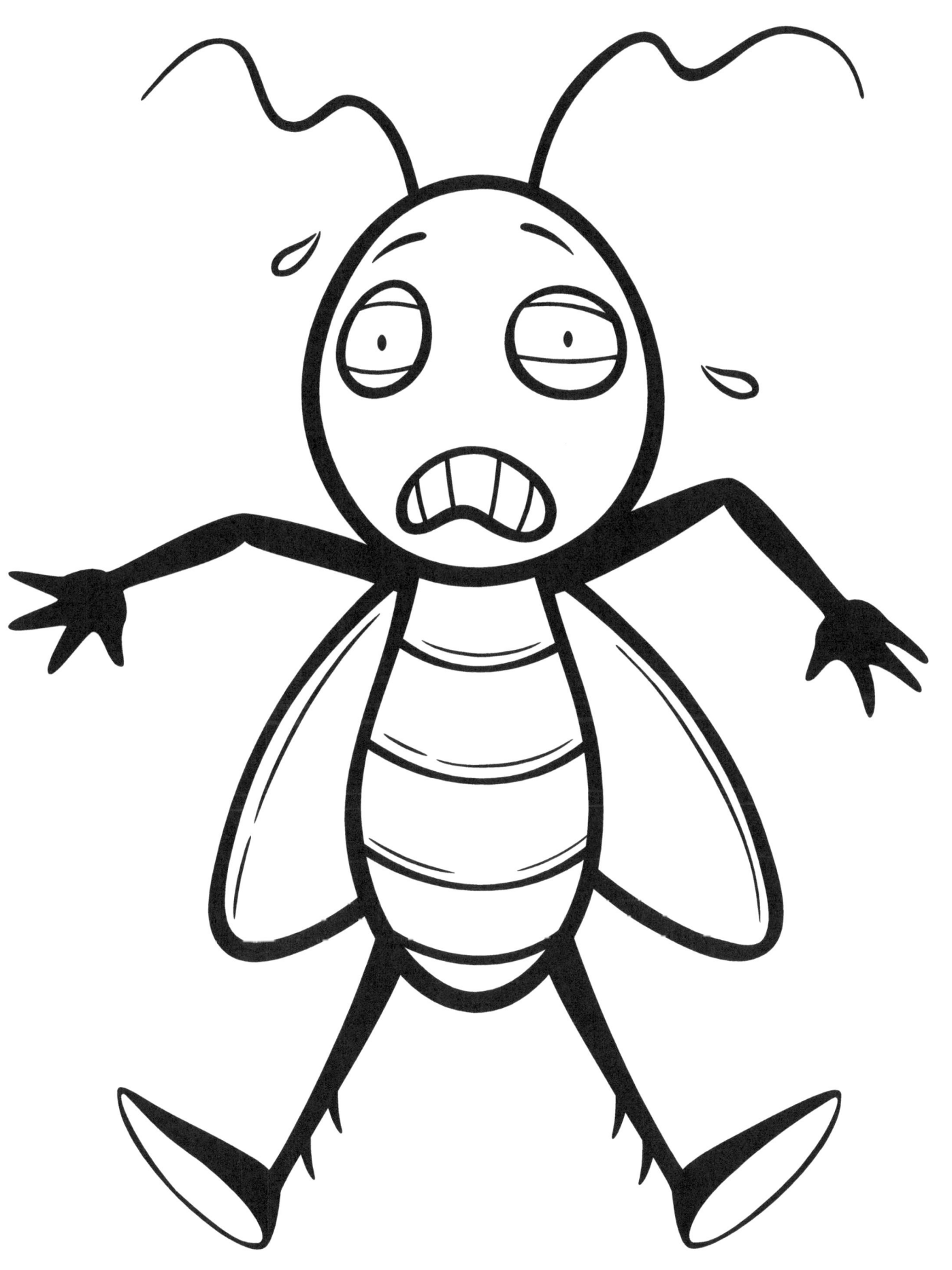

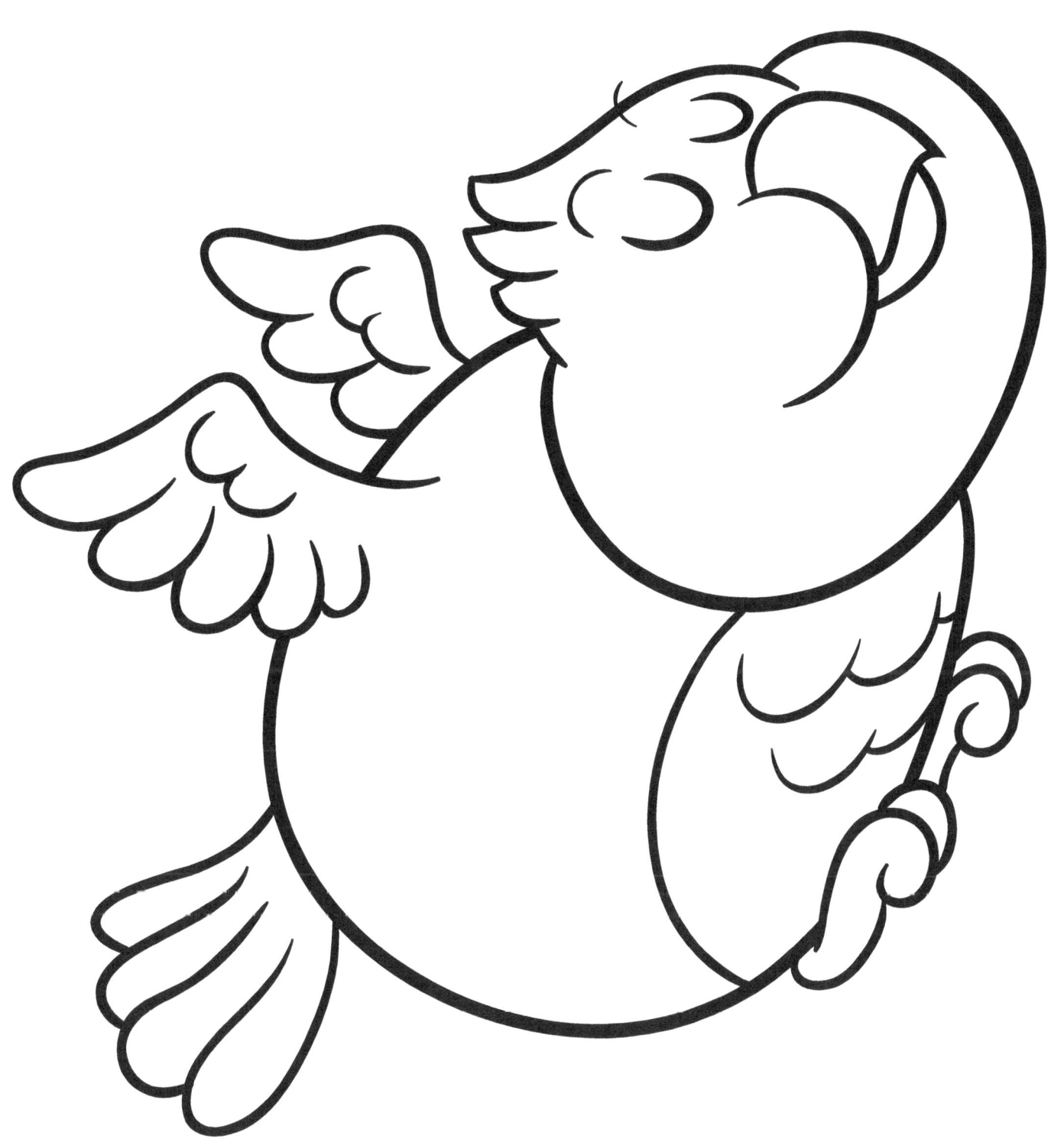

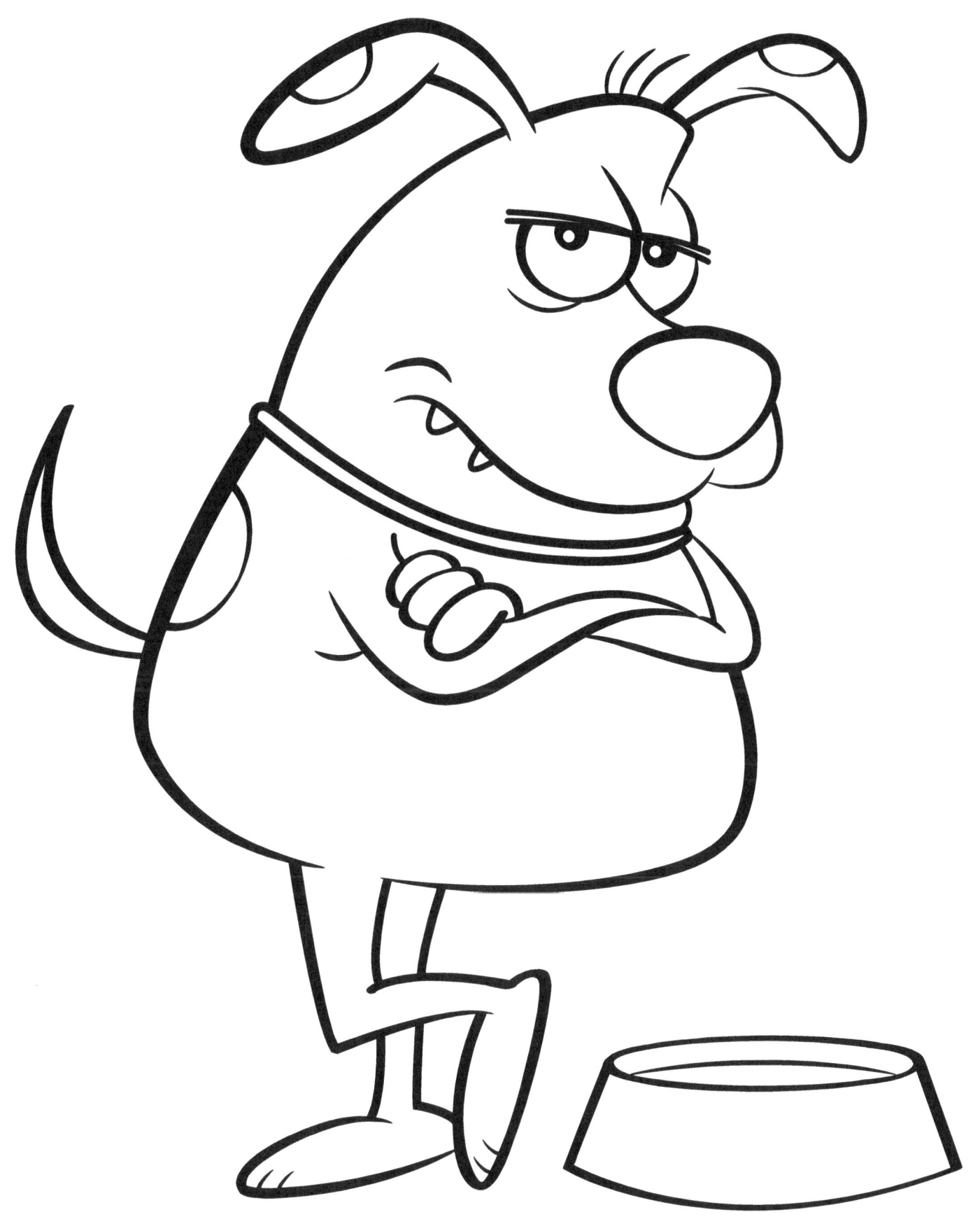

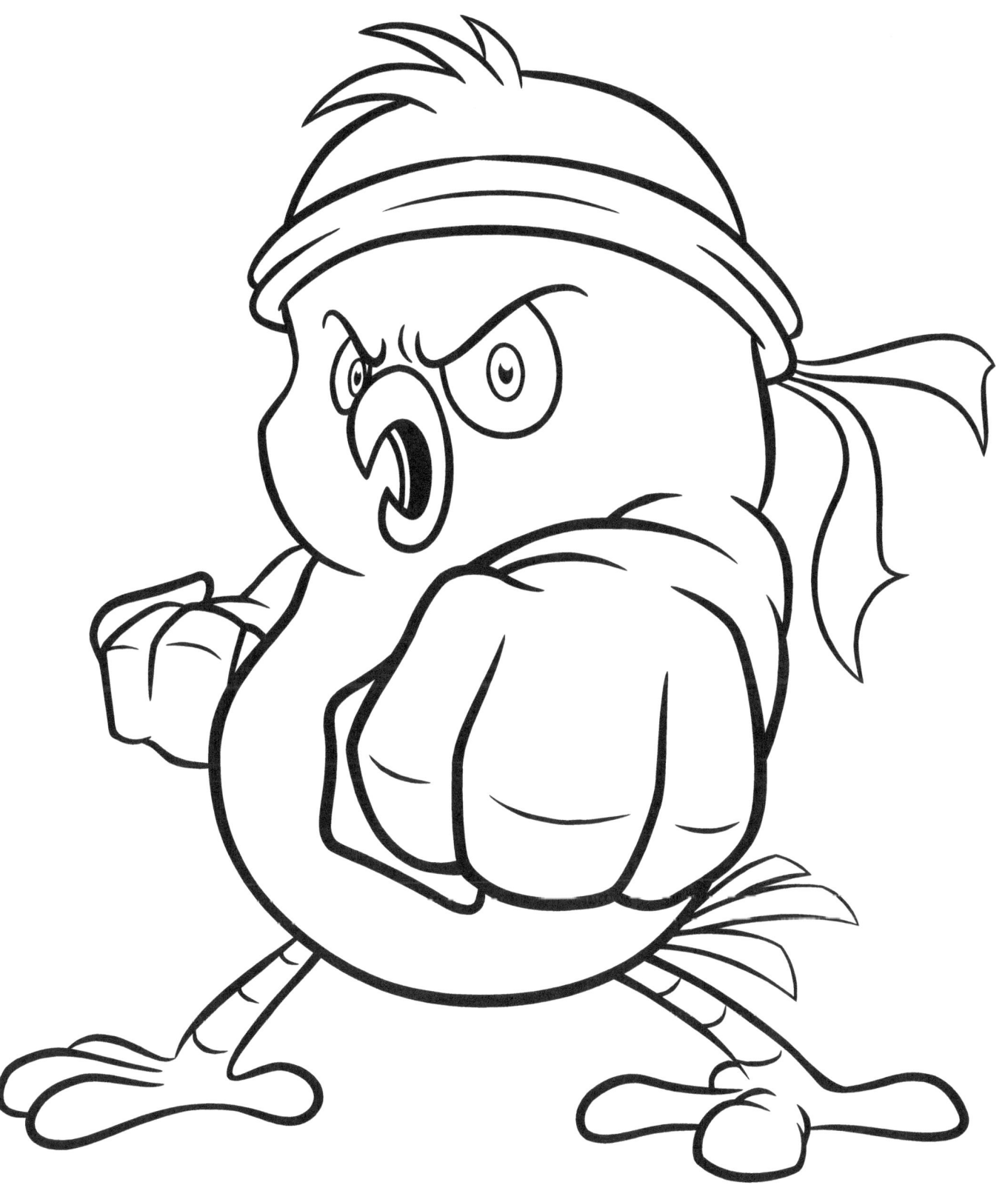

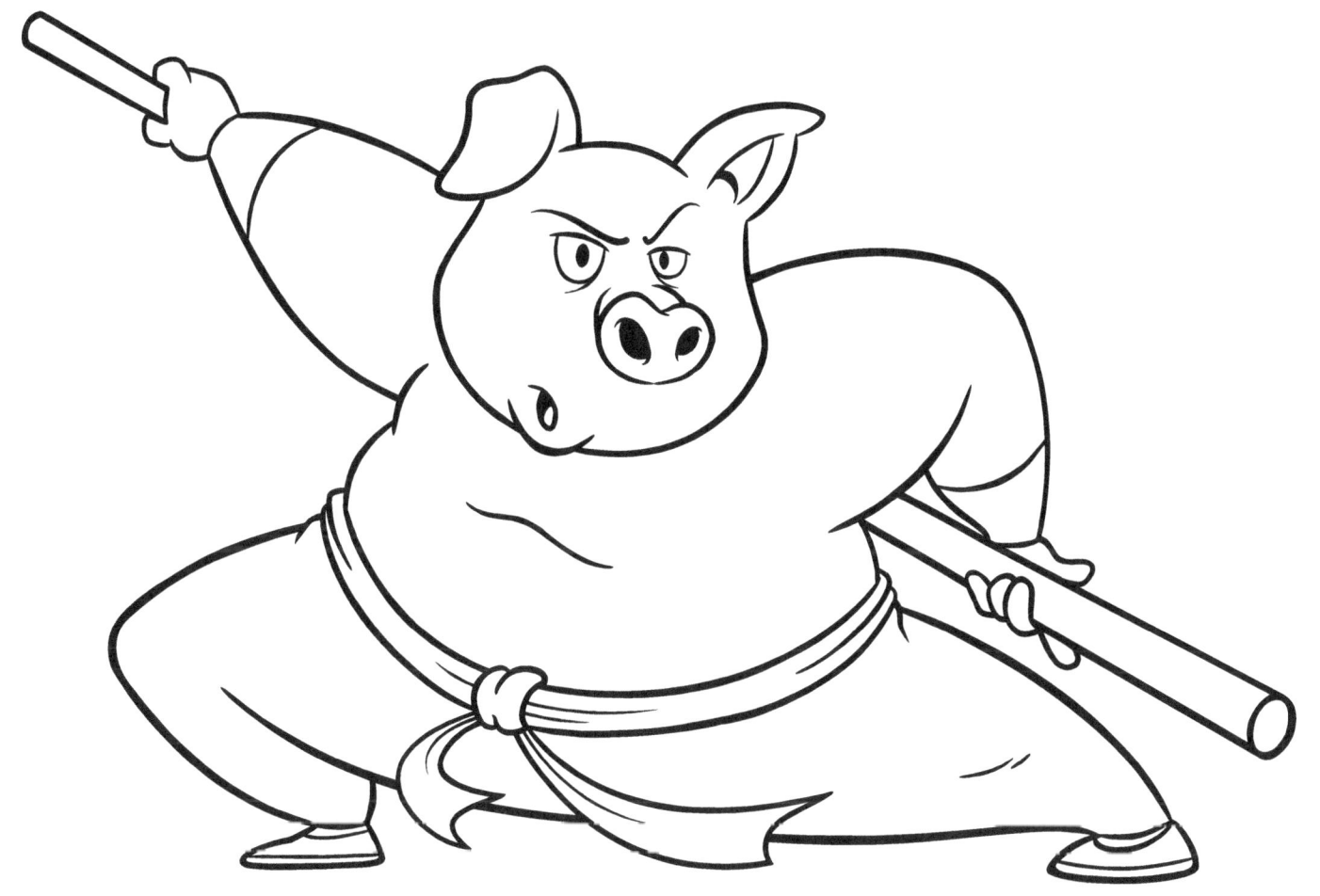

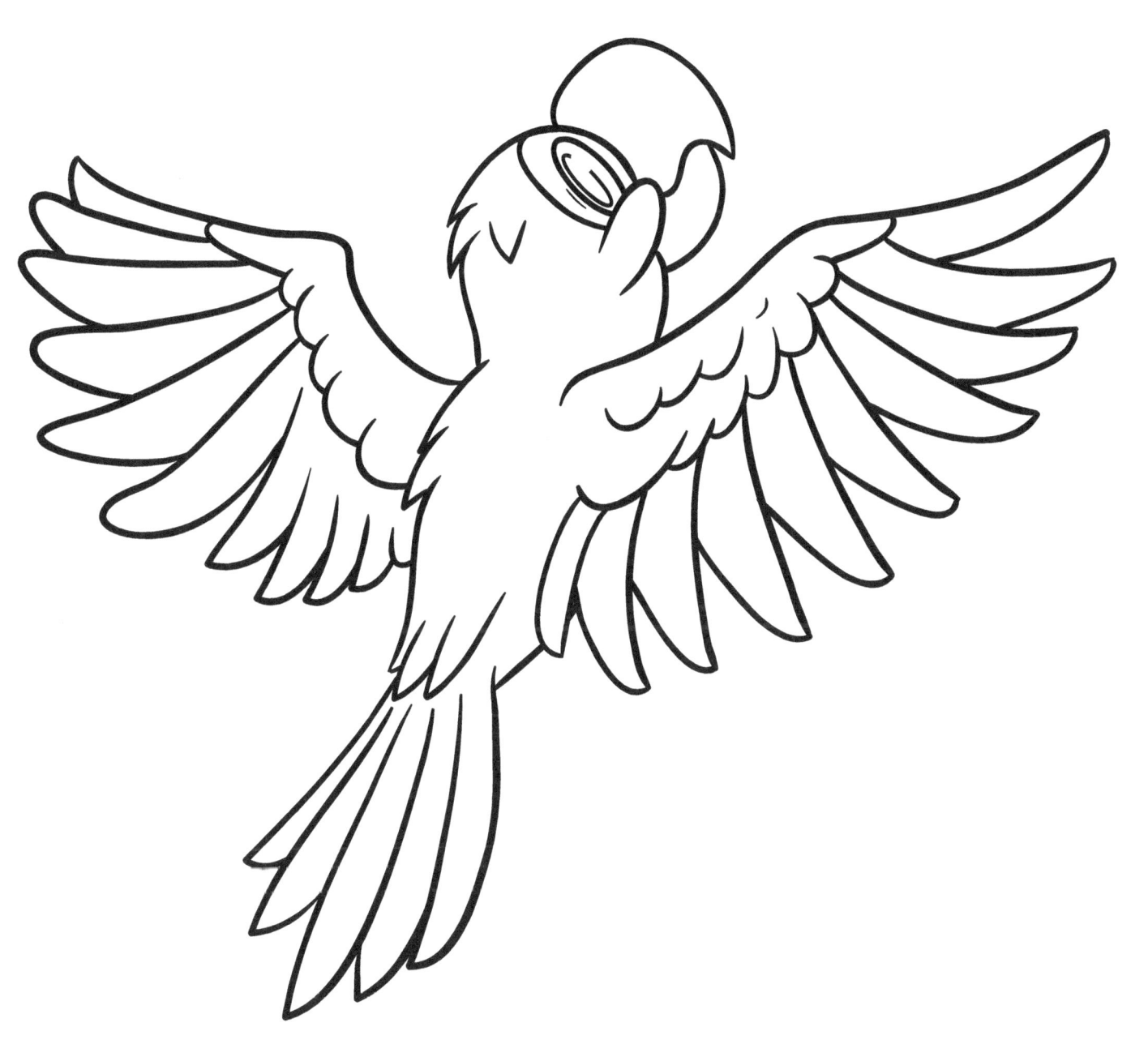

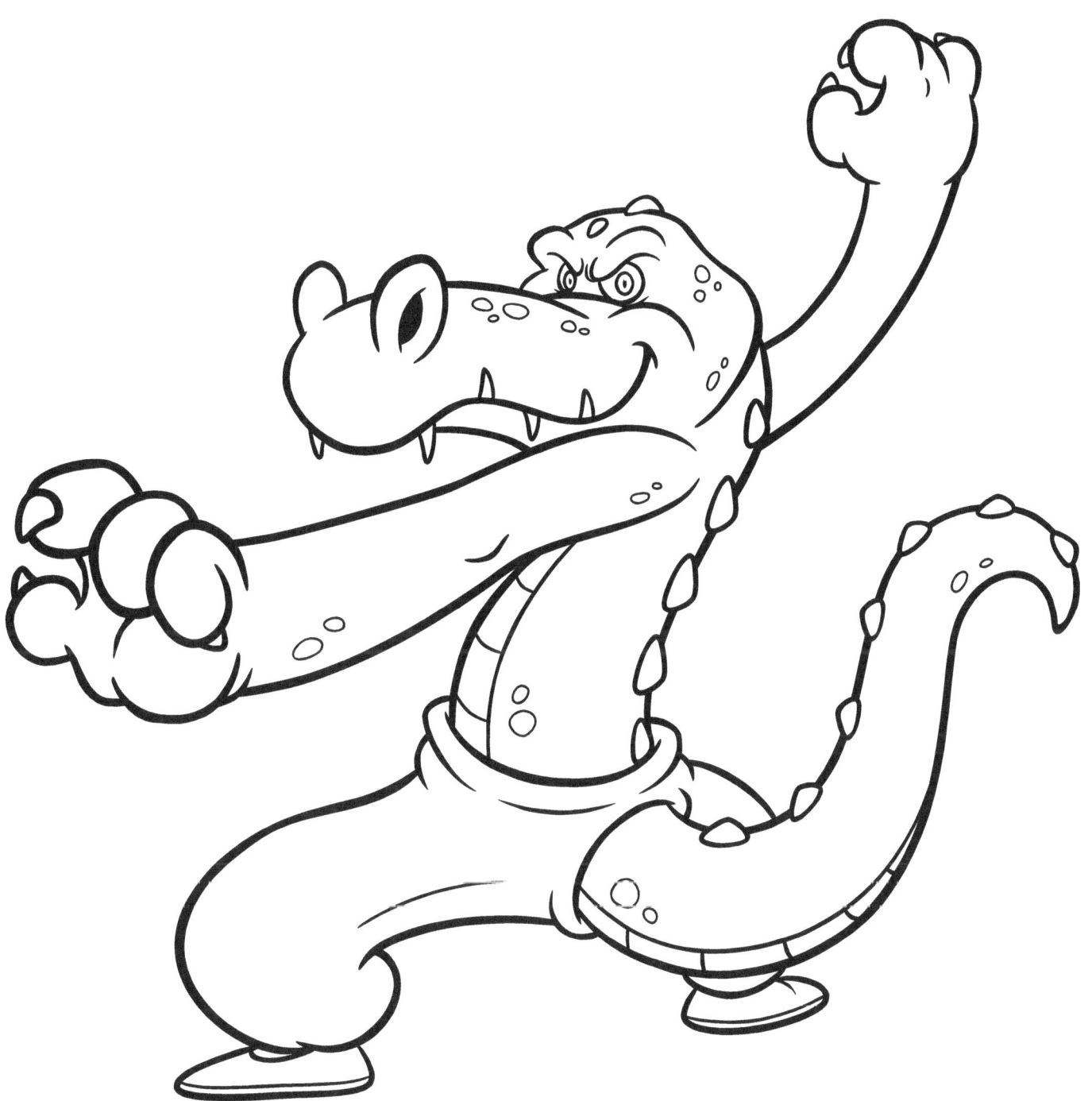

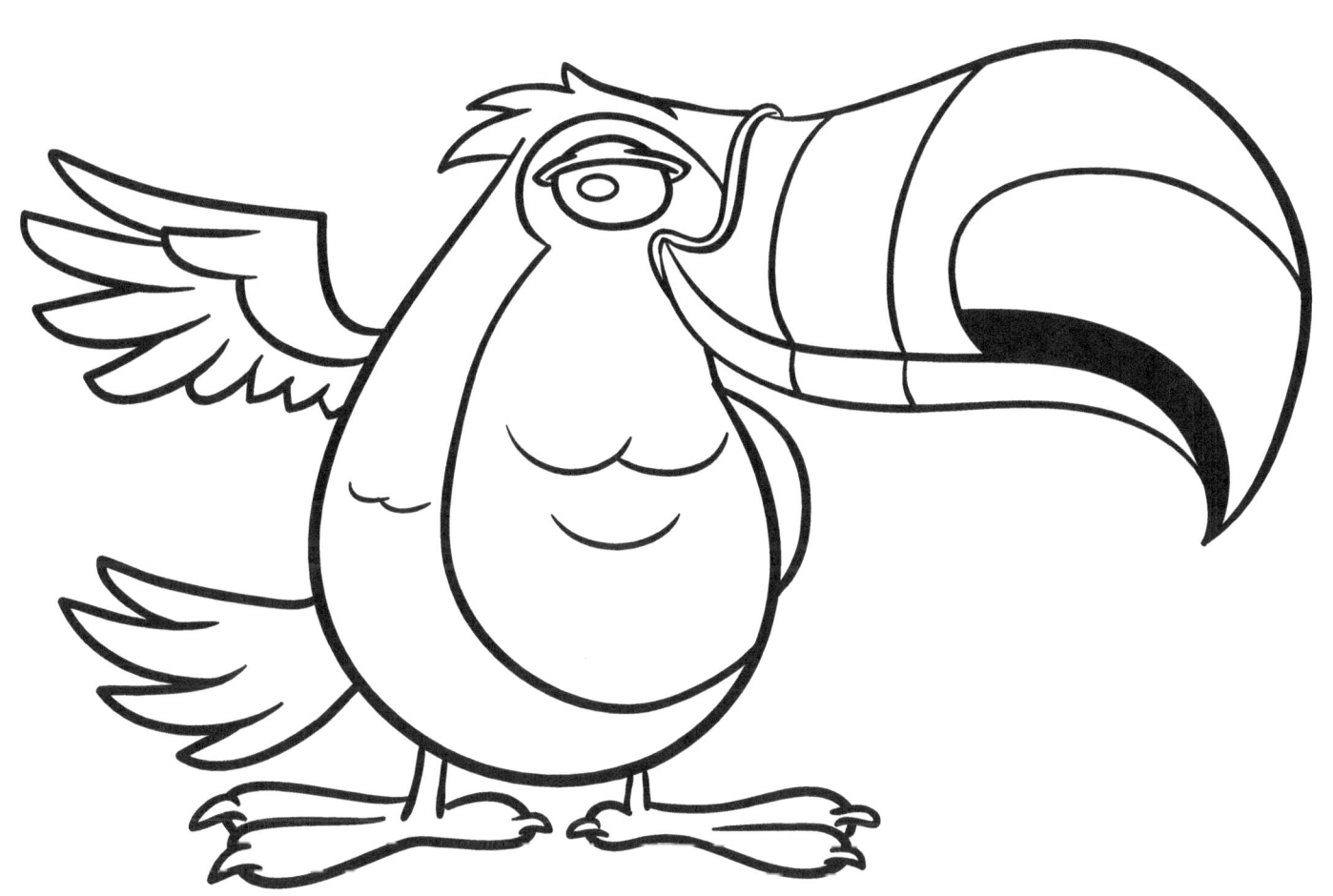

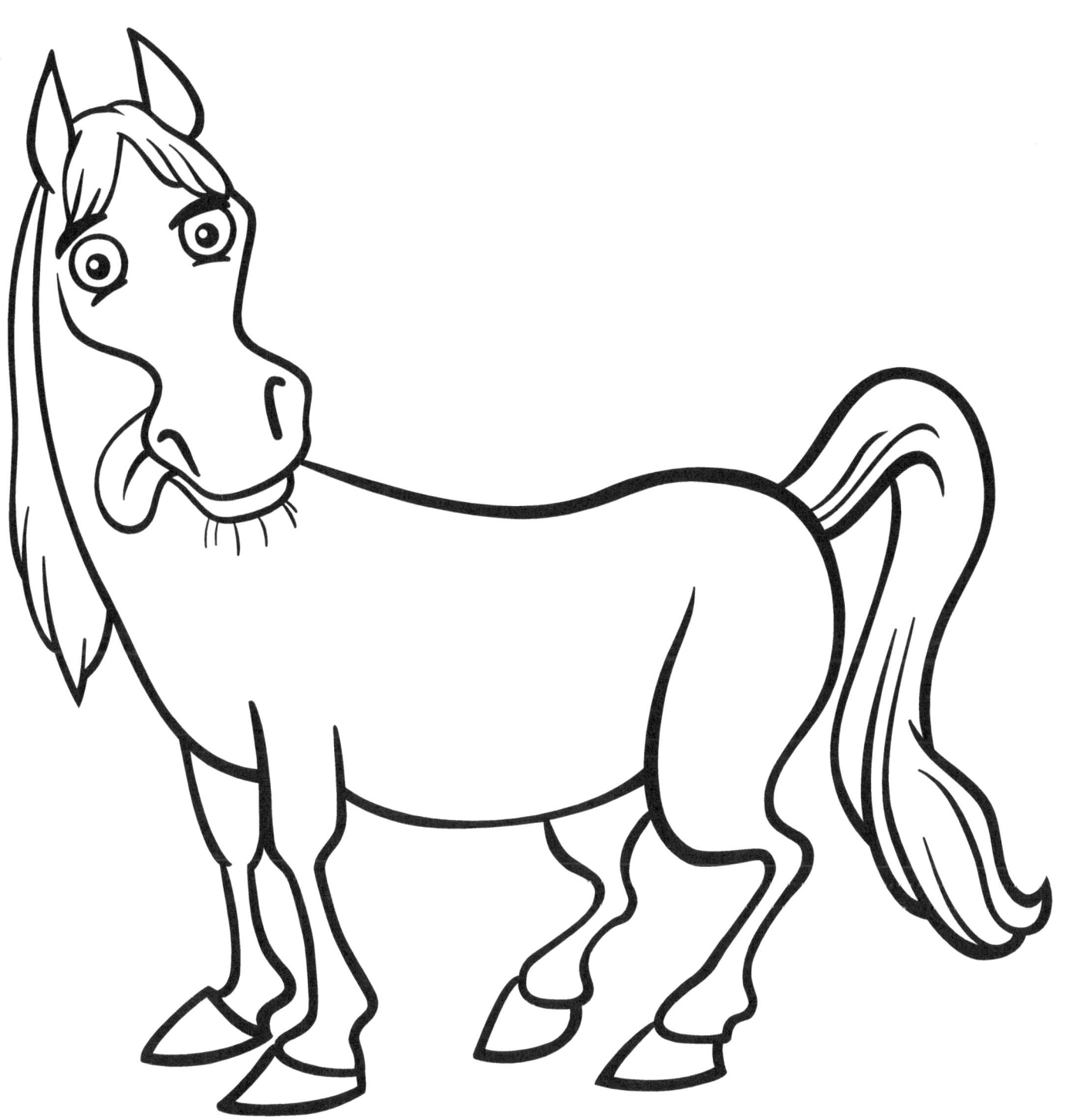

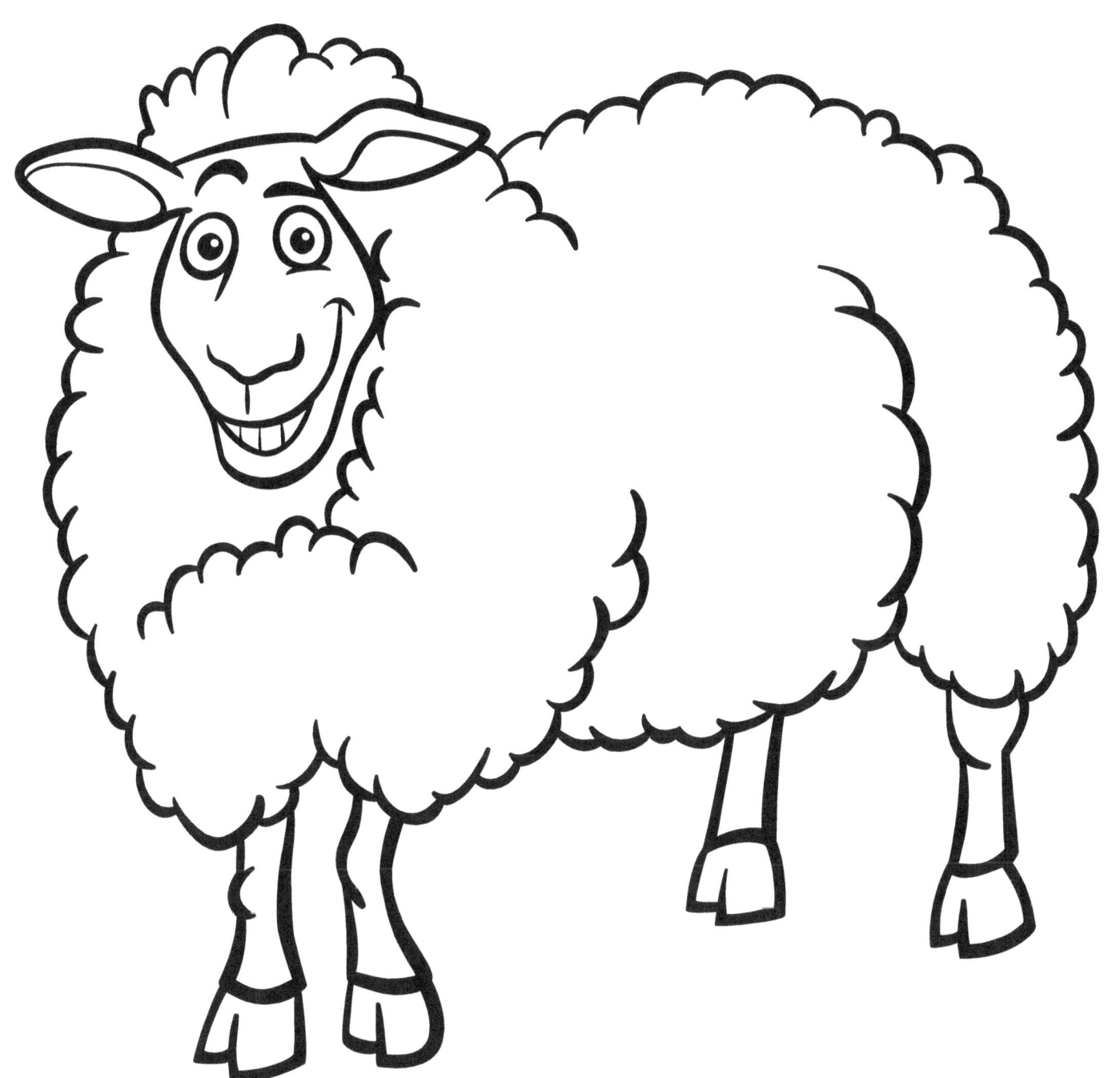

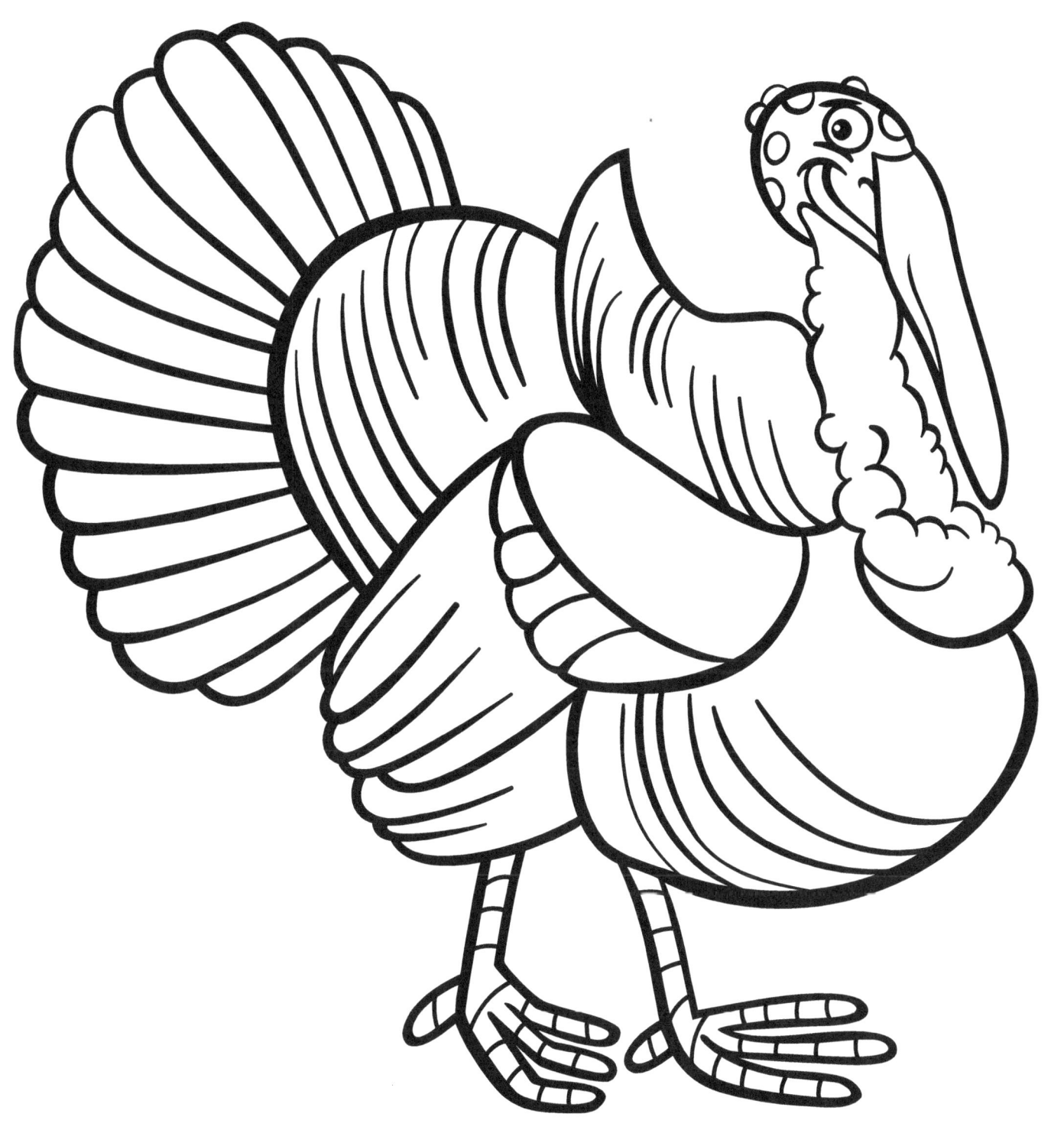

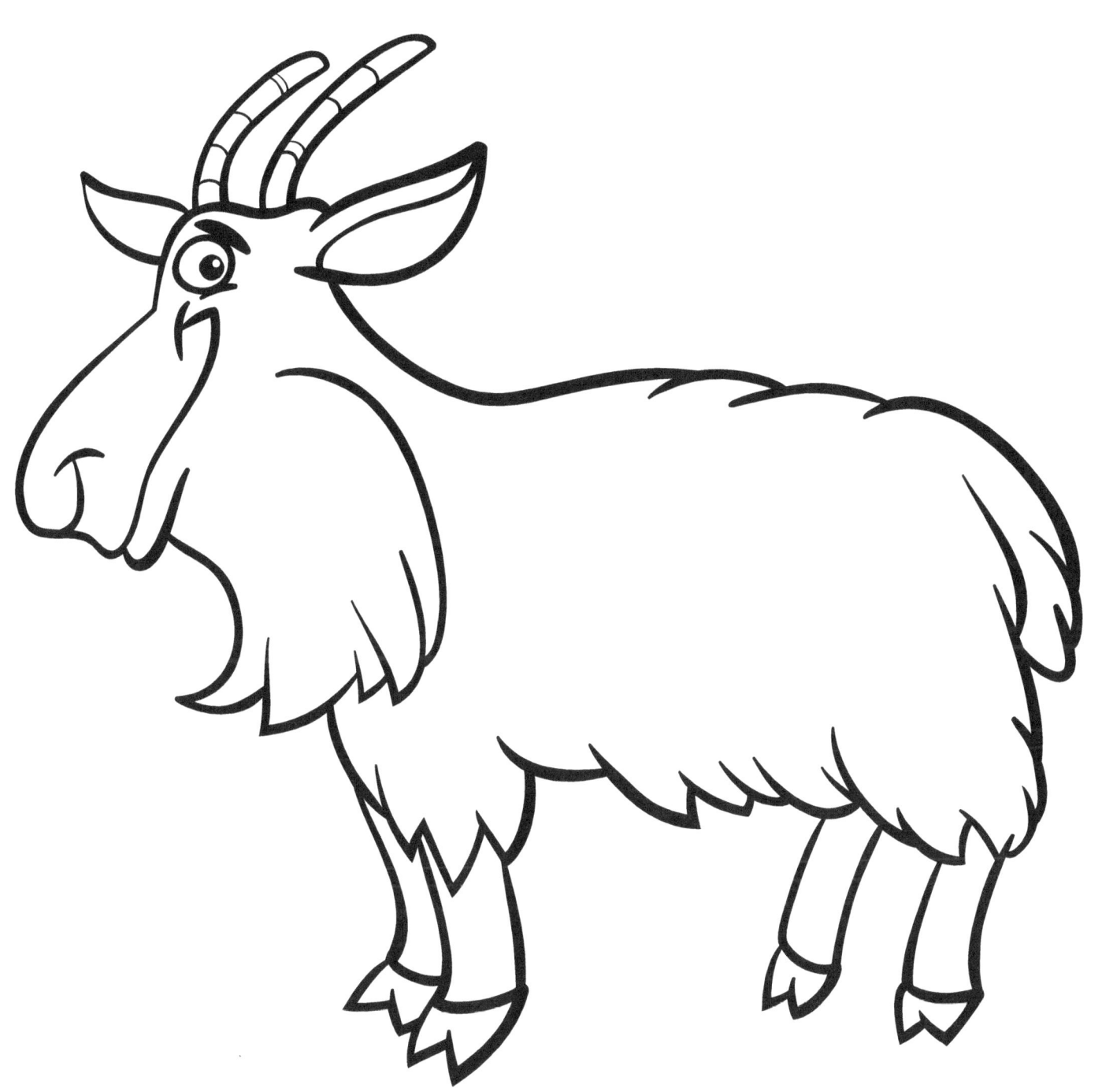

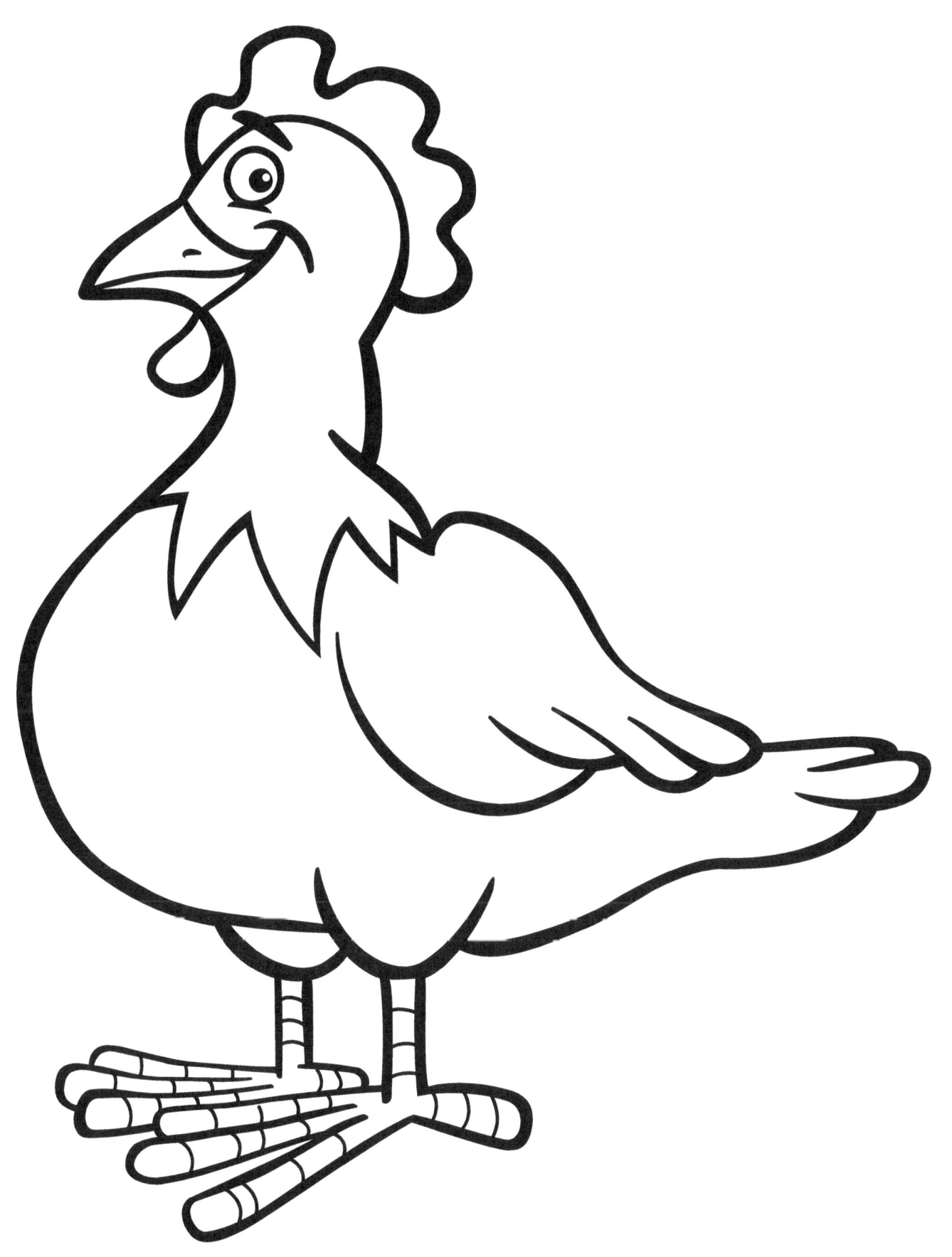

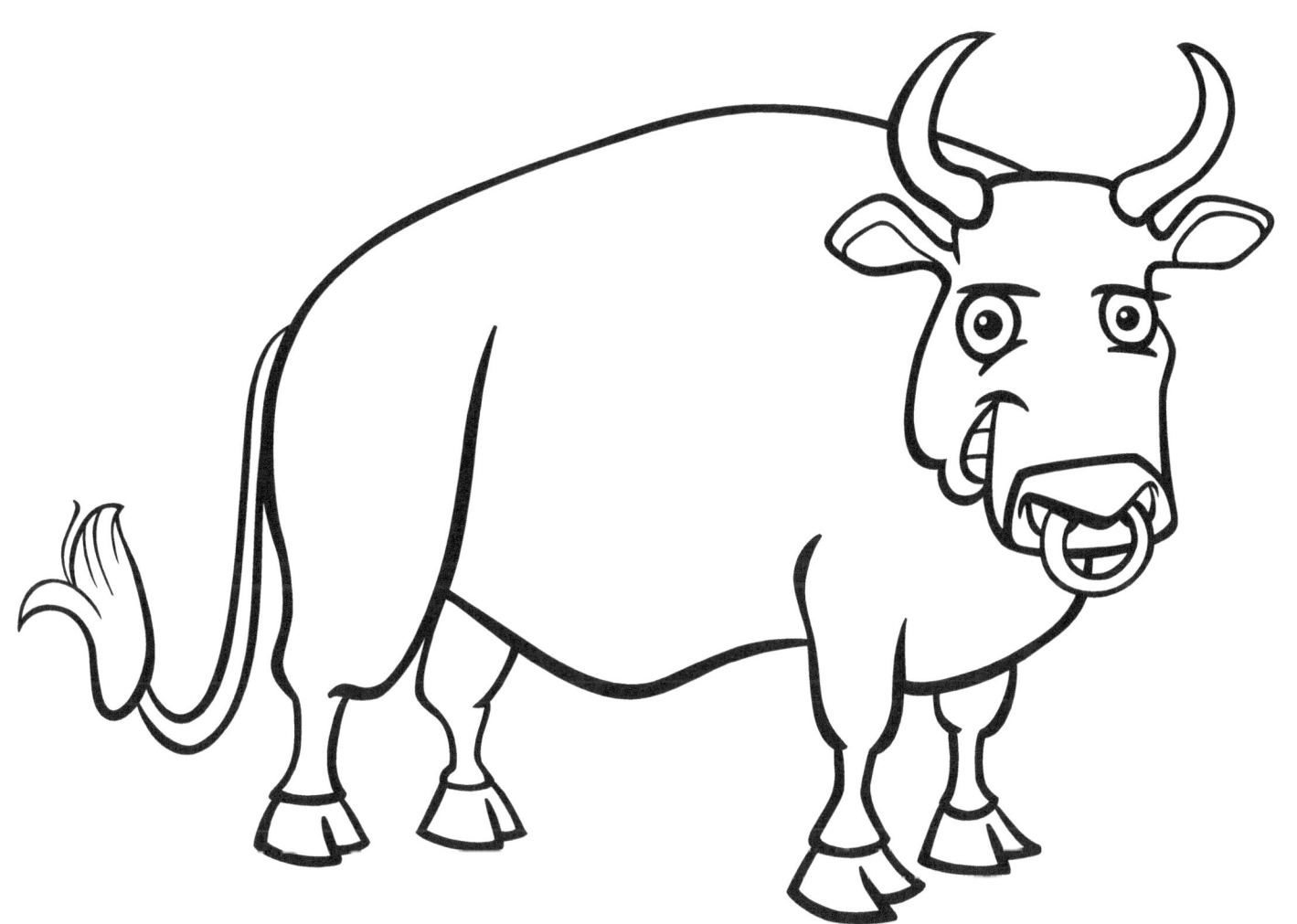

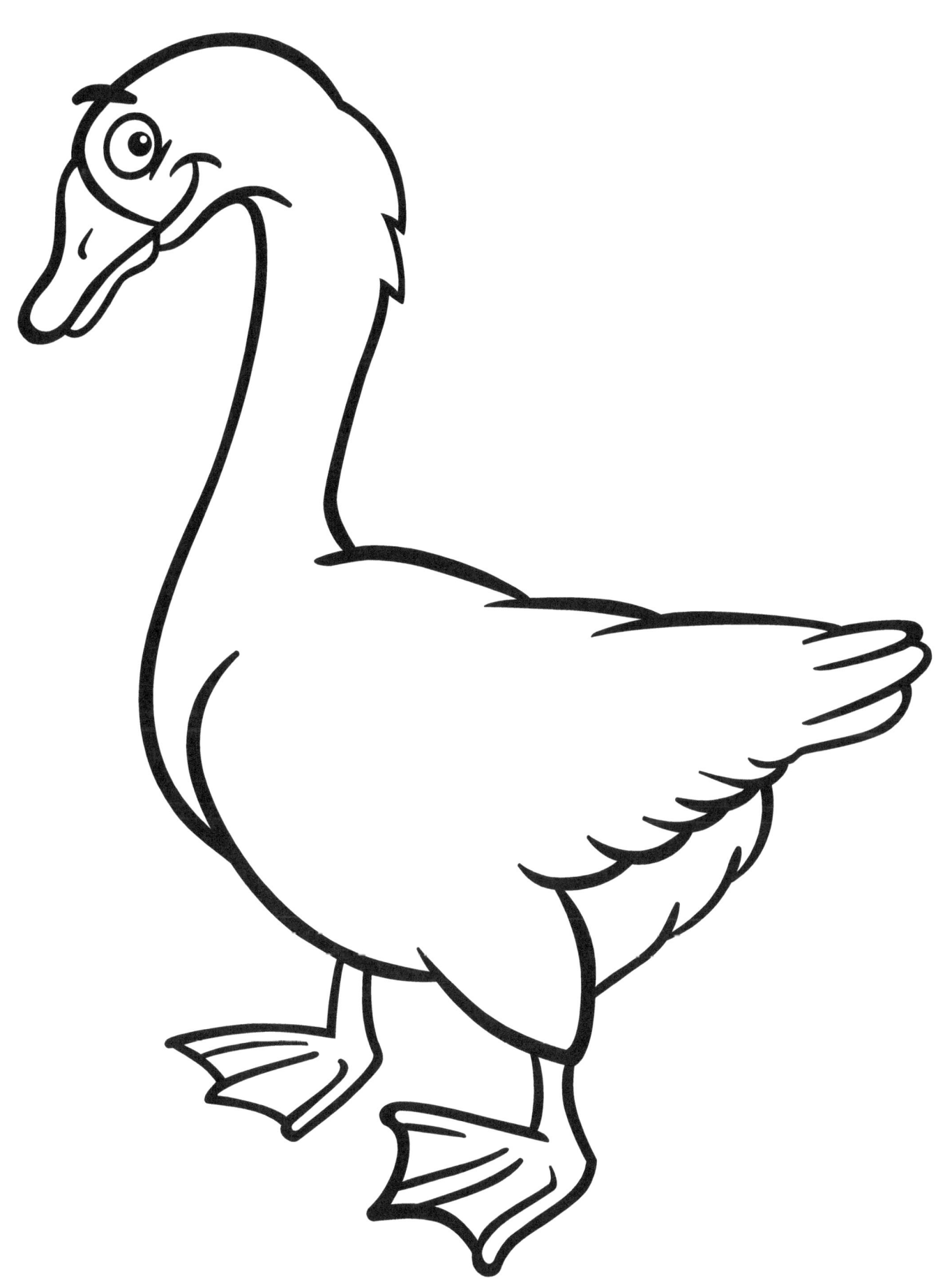

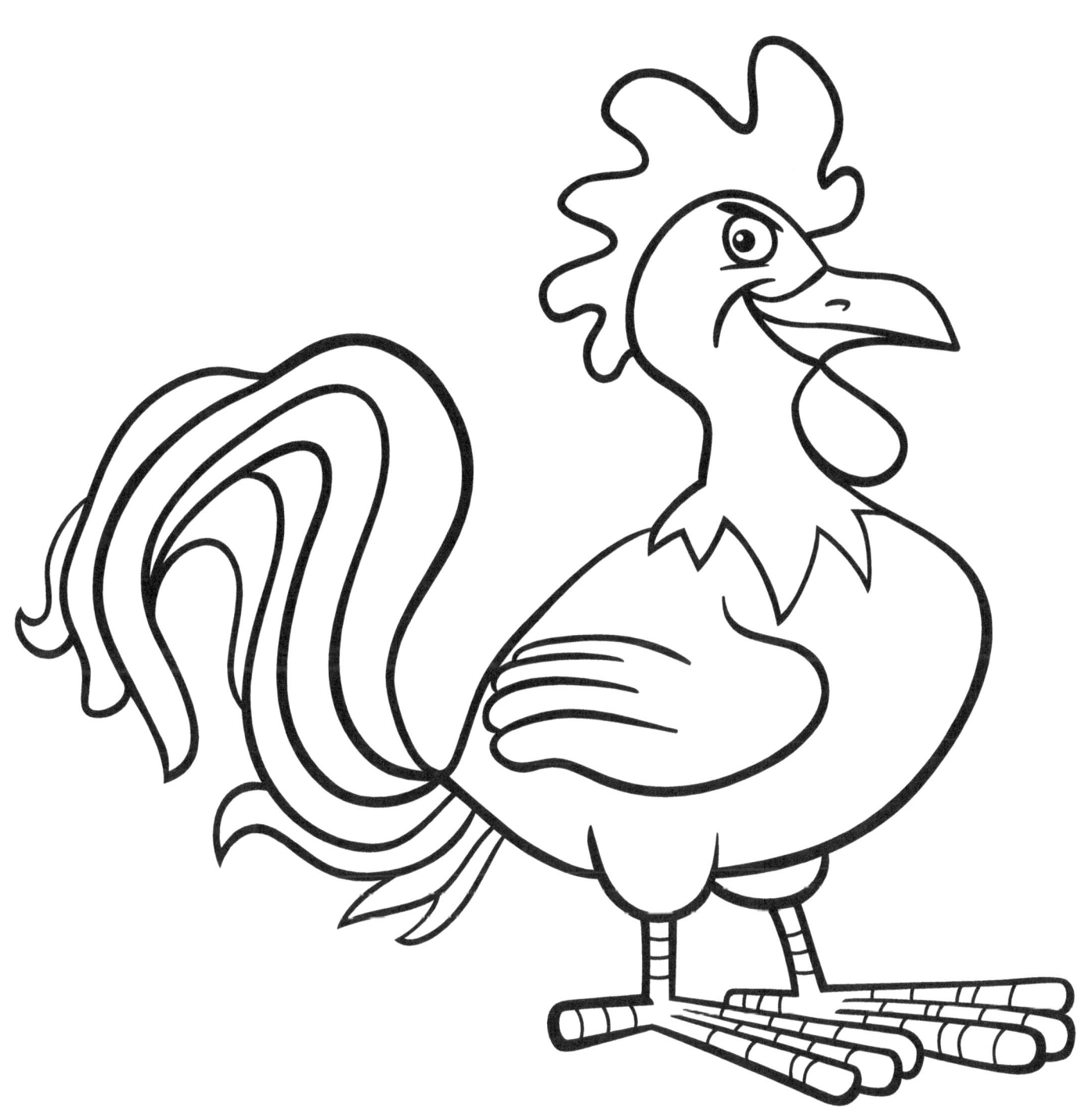

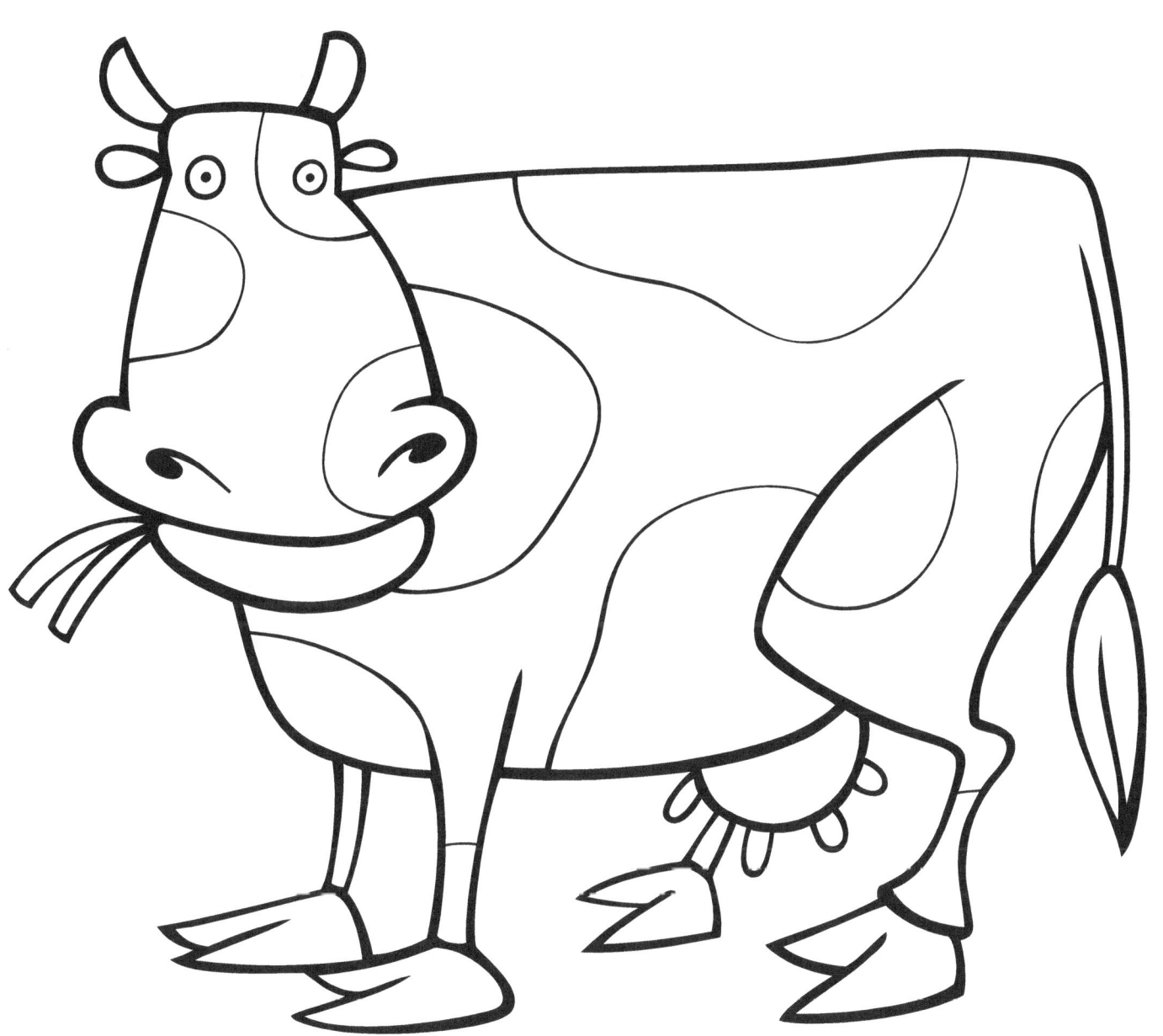

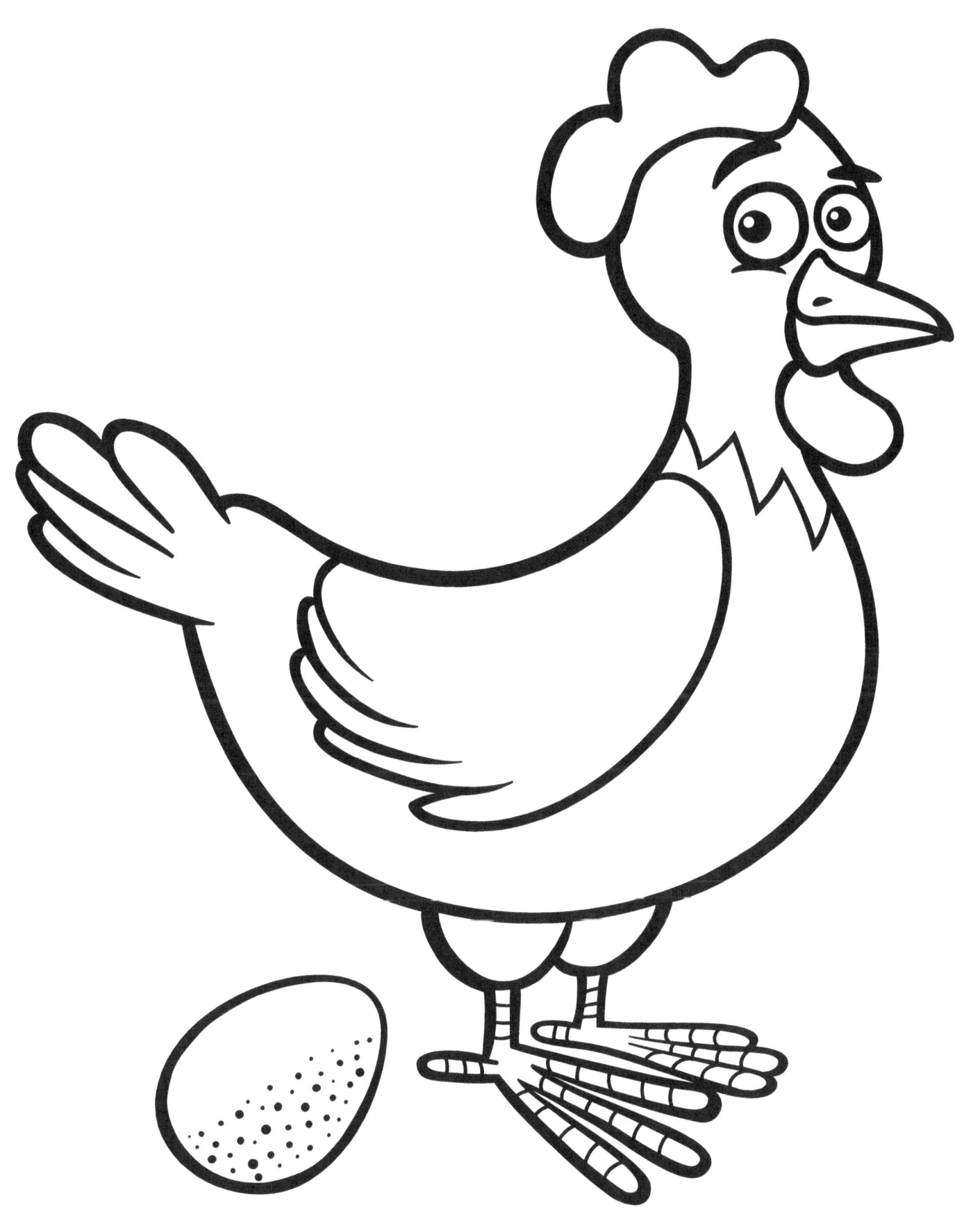

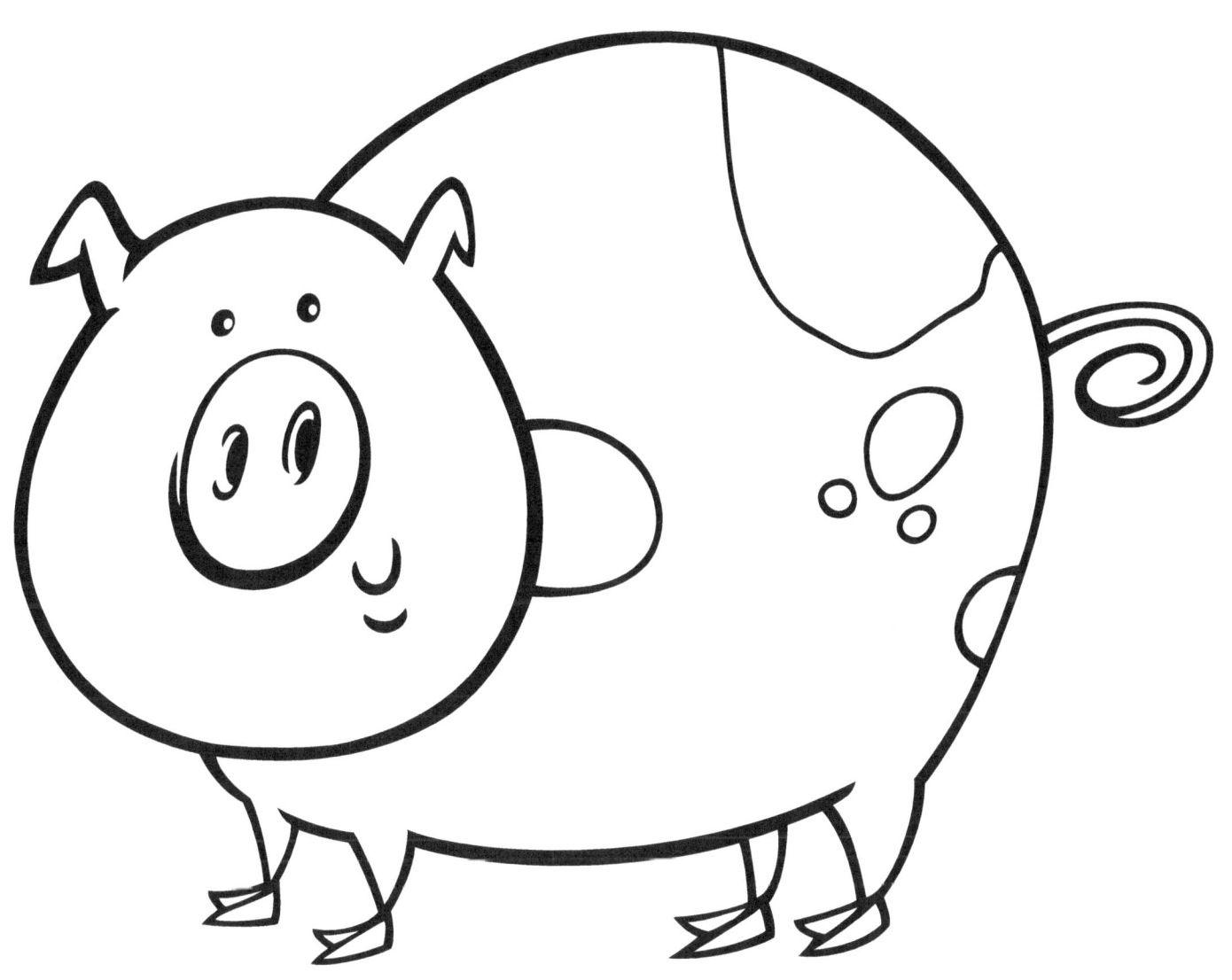

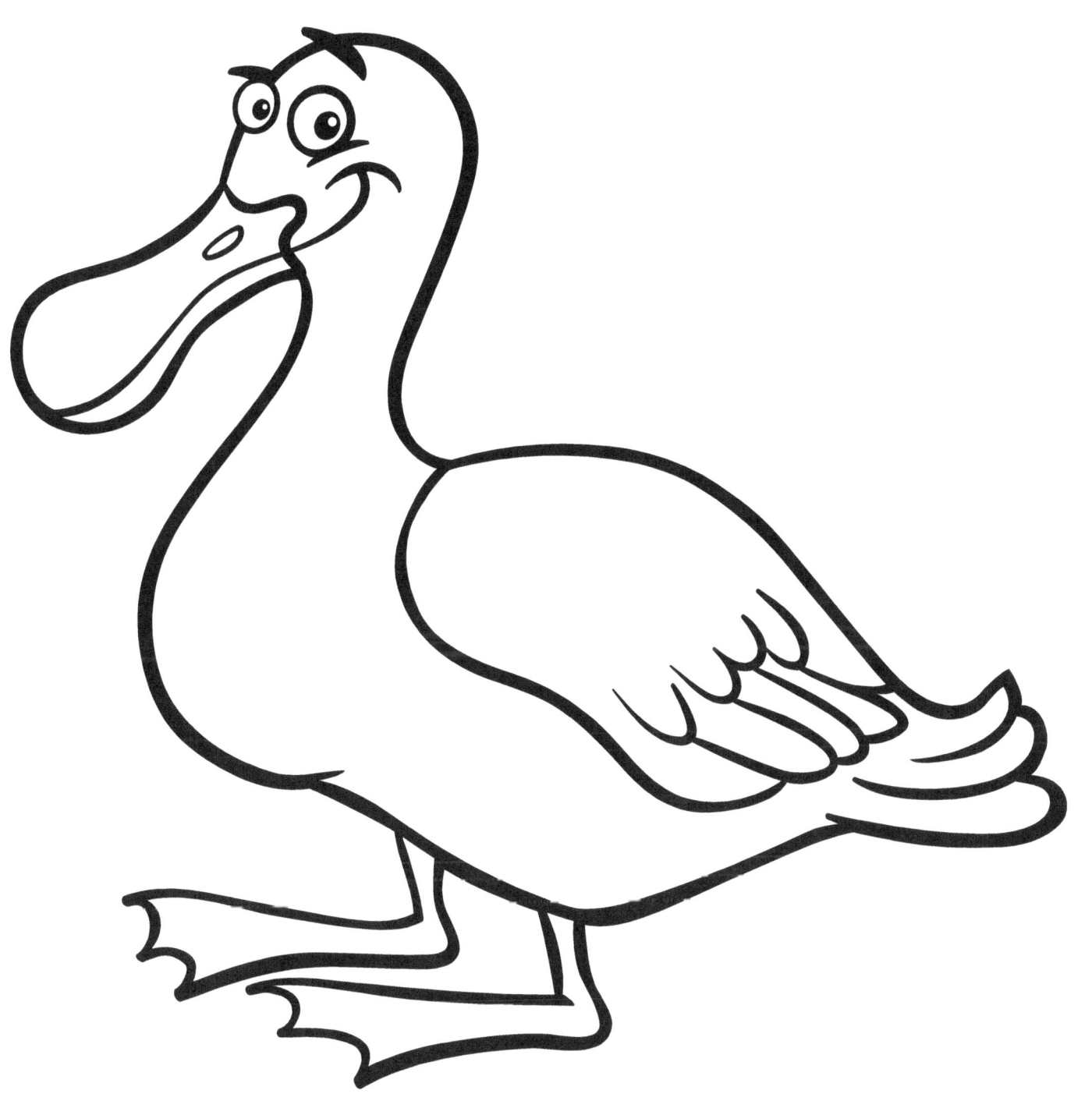

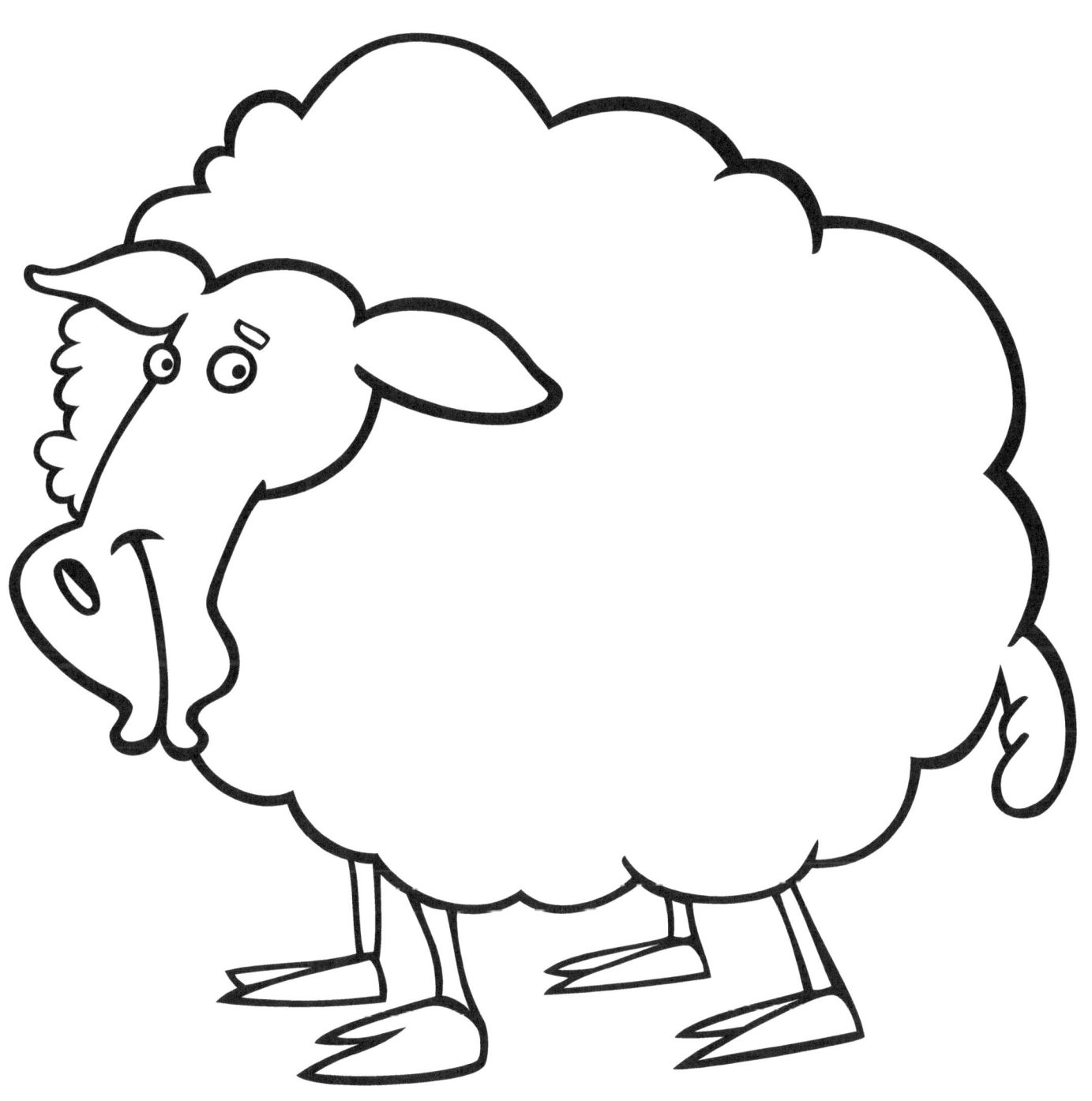

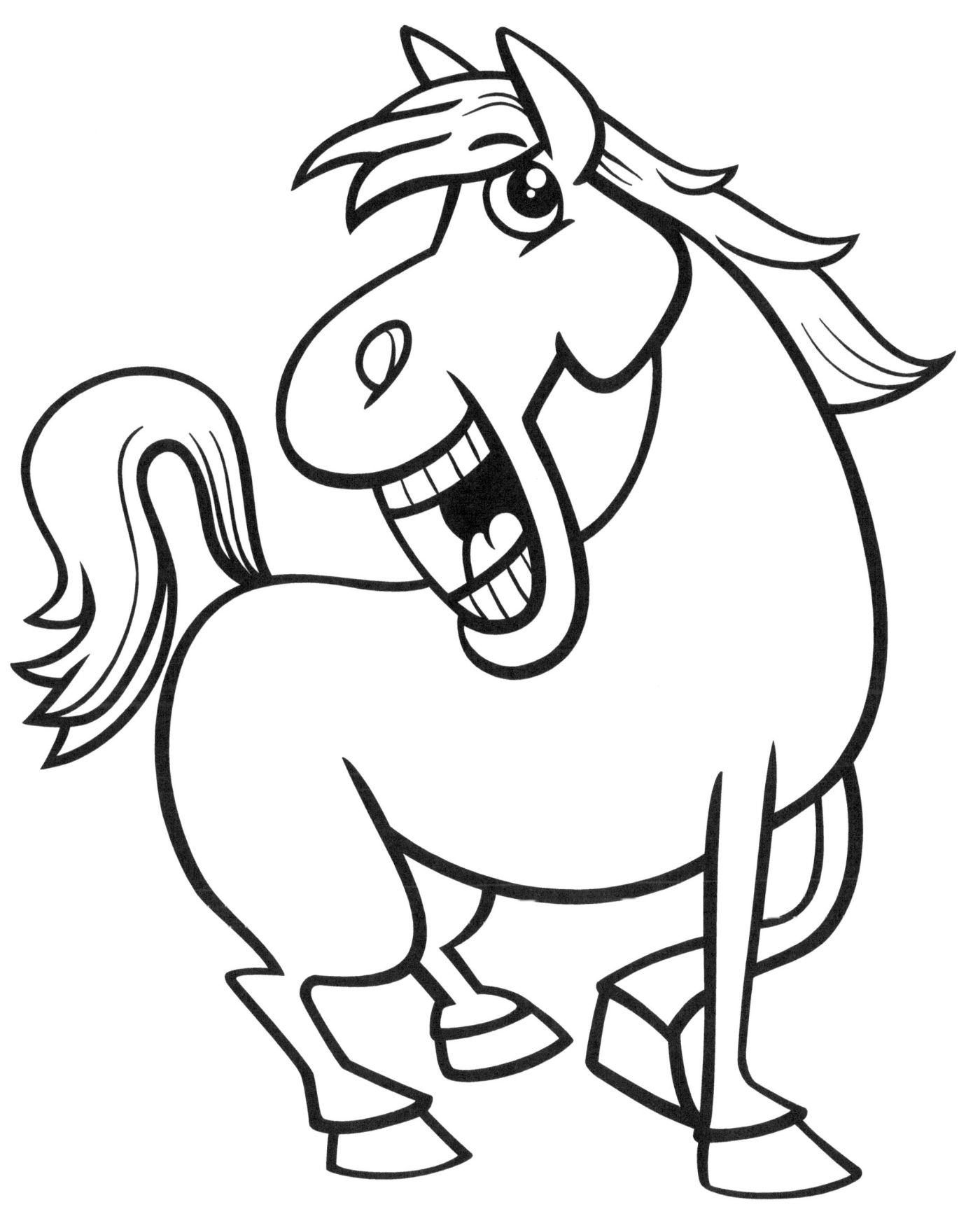

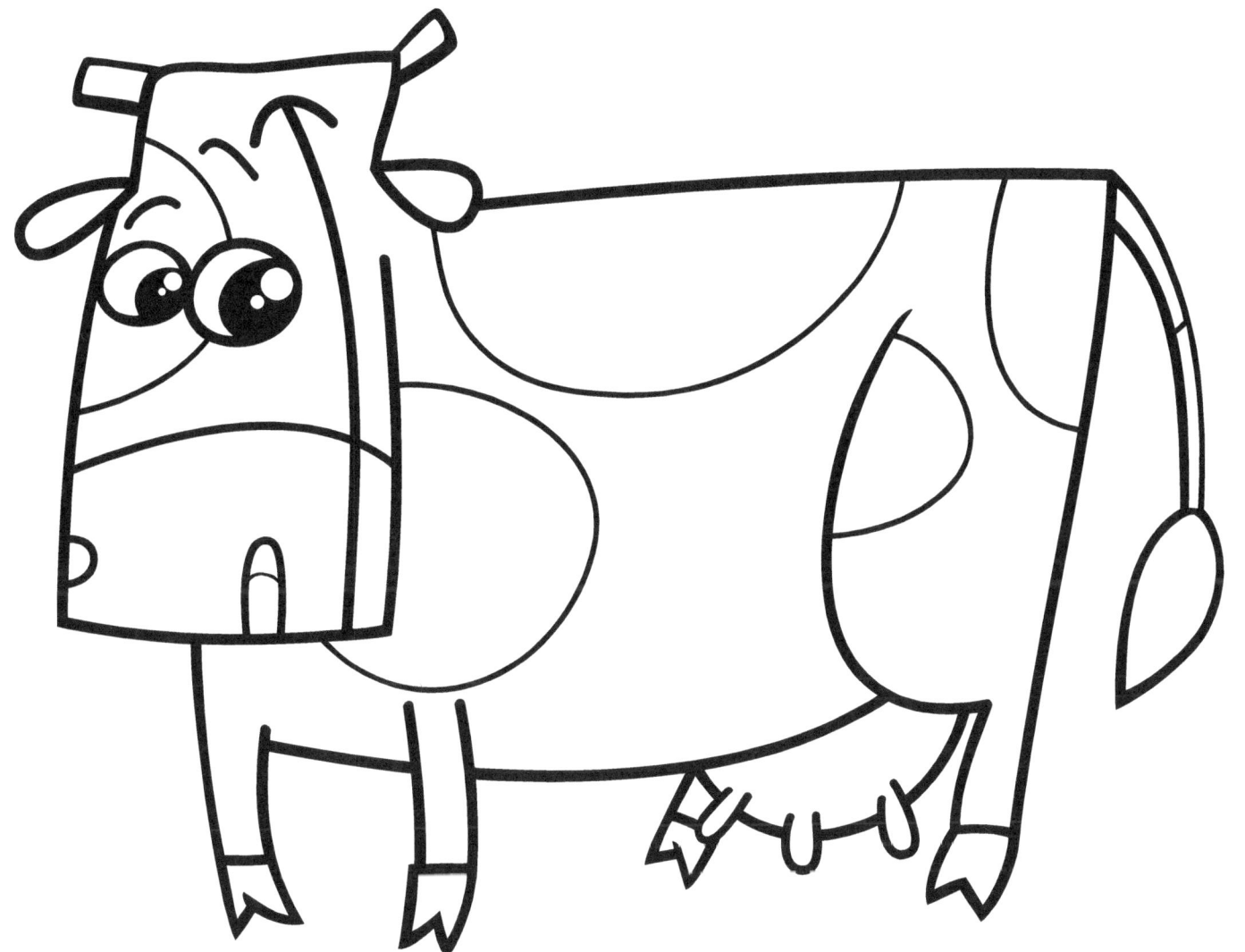

Coloring Book for Kids
50 Funny Animals

Published by:
Art Therapy Coloring
www.arttherapycoloring.com

Images Under License From Shutterstock

www.ingramcontent.com/pod-product-compliance
Lightning Source LLC
Chambersburg PA
CBHW081342180526
45171CB00006B/586